THE DUPLEX

By Ed Bullins

THE DUPLEX

A Black Love Fable in Four Movements

WILLIAM MORROW AND COMPANY, INC.   NEW YORK   1971

Printed in the United States of America

Library of Congress Catalog Card Number 70–132162

Designed by Terry Reid

To Robert Macbeth
and the New Lafayette Theatre

THE DUPLEX

The Duplex: A Black Love Fable in Four Movements was pre-
sented at the New Lafayette Theatre in Harlem from May 22 to
June 5, 1970. The production was directed by Robert Macbeth. The
stage manager was V. Rachman Cyrille; sets and lighting were
by Ademola Olugbefola, James and Tobias Macbeth, and Morgan
Morris. The cast was as follows:

CHARACTER	ACTOR
Steve Benson	Roscoe Orman
Velma Best	Roberta Raysor
O. D. Best	Sonny Jim
Marco Polo Henderson	Bill Lathan
Montgomery Henderson	Whitman Mayo
Tootsie Franklin	George Miles
Mamma	Estelle Evans
Pops	Chief Bey
Sister Sukie	Yvette Hawkins
Wanda	Silvia Sims
Crook	Gary Bolling
Marie Horton	Rosanna Carter

Musicians:

Vocal	Helen Ellis
Flute	Sonny Morgan
Bass	Nagi
Mamalukelbi Kembel Taiyba Kuna	Nadi Qamar
Drums	Richard Landrum

The People

STEVE BENSON *26 years old.*

VELMA BEST *24 years old. Dark, shapely.*

O. D. BEST *28 years old. Medium height, but powerfully muscled.* VELMA'S *husband.*

MARCO POLO HENDERSON *27 years old. Light skinned, with curly hair.*

TOOTSIE FRANKLIN *24 years old. Tall, dark and lanky.*

MONTGOMERY HENDERSON *46 years old. Tall and lean.* MARCO'S *father.*

MAMMA *An old woman. The neighborhood drunk.*

POPS *An old man.* MAMMA'S *current man.*

SISTER SUKIE *22 years old.* VELMA'S *friend.*

WANDA *20 years old.* MARCO'S *girl.*

CROOK *22 years old.* O.D.'S *buddy.*

MARIE HORTON *44 years old.* WANDA'S *aunt.*

First Movement

YOU GOTTA BE MAH MAN, MAN

Dark
Loneliness
Pain
Dark
Be mine

Hope
Despair
Cold
Man
You gotta be mah man
man

Sweat
Heat
Fire
Hate
Move in me

Blood
Spit
Funk
Shit
You gotta be mah man
man

Work
Ach
AAAAAAAAIIIIIII
My man
my love
don't go

Black
Female
Pussy
Love
You gotta be mah man
man

SCENE 1

The people in this play are Black.

TIME
Early 1960's.

SCENE
A Southern California duplex.

A cutaway view of a building having a flat on the first floor and one on the second. Or a nonrealistic setting, suggesting same.

Or the different playing areas can be staged on various levels.

To the right, the stairway or ramp runs from the stage to the second floor of the duplex. This is the front stairway. Upon the landing of the second floor are the doors to the upstairs bathroom and STEVE BENSON's *room. On the left of the stage, a winding set of stairs acts as the back staircase.*

Downstairs: two rooms. To the right, next to the stairs and the short hallway to the outside, is the bedroom of VELMA *and* O. D. BEST. *Next to it is the living room with its archway leading to the downstairs kitchen and adjoining rooms.*

Upstairs: three rooms can be seen. STEVE BENSON's *room is above the* BESTS', *then* MARCO POLO HENDERSON's, *and a tiny kitchen from which the backstairs lead downward.*

The card games on the second floor are held in MARCO's *room. It has a table, several chairs, a bed and other small pieces of furniture.*

STEVE BENSON's *room has a couch which makes up into a bed, a bookcase, filled with paperbacks, a chair, a reading lamp and a low table.*

Each room and the stairways have various doors which lead to rooms, closets and enclosures in the interior of the house. The set should suggest one of those bizarre structures from a gone period of Southern California antiquity, with pompous cornices, chimneys without sources and fireplaces without chimneys. There are exposed beams on the first floor, supporting low ceilings. Separately, the rooms and stairways are painted and decorated in multiple hues; it would seem that the more imaginative in-

mates of an institution for the insane planned the décor: the BESTS' *bedroom is immodest crimson; their living room is yellow green;* MARCO POLO HENDERSON's *room is orange; the stairways do not matter except that the frayed carpeting on the front staircase is red.*

At curtain rise, the building is darkened. Not black, for the rooms' shadowy depths have varied tones and textures.

Footsteps are heard upon the cement walk out front, then the hollow clumping of one person's feet climbing several wooden steps and then their crossing the porch.

A figure enters and starts up the front stairs. VELMA BEST *turns her reading lamp on. In the dim light she can be seen leaning from the edge of her bed, straining to hear the footfalls. She swings out of bed and goes to the hall door but does not open it. Through her nightgown her shape is full, womanly; she is a very dark, voluptuous woman.*

The figure enters the bathroom and closes the door. Light is seen from around the door; water is heard splashing from a faucet.

Downstairs, VELMA BEST *climbs back into bed and switches the light off.*

The light upstairs goes out in the bathroom and the figure comes out and enters STEVE BENSON's *room.*

Gradually lights come up on MARCO'S *room and the recording "After Hours" is heard softly in the background.* MARCO, TOOTSIE FRANKLIN *and* MONTGOMERY HENDERSON *sit around the table playing cards.*

MONTGOMERY (*Challenges*)
Gawd damn, boy, sonna ah bitch if'n I won't!

TOOTSIE (*Voice rises weirdly, musically*)
Heee heee . . . Oh Lawdy . . . Look ah hare at what dis man's got!

MARCO (*Low and muttered disgust*)
A double run. Ah gawd damn . . . sheet . . . matha . . .

(STEVE *enters.* MARCO *poorly mimics a Southern drawl.*)

Wahl, if'n it ain't Stevie Bent-tan . . . mah old wanderin' roommate.

(MARCO *is wearing a ten-gallon straw hat, shorts and white woolen socks.*)

STEVE
Hey, Marc, what's happen'n, man?

TOOTSIE
How's it goin', Steve?

STEVE (*Walks to table*)
Hi, Tootsie. . . . How's it goin', man?
(*Turns to* MONTGOMERY HENDERSON)
And hey, Montgomery!

MONTGOMERY

Wahl, mah little short son's come home.

(*With a dour expression upon face*)

Son . . . dese hare brothers of yourn are gettin' the old man's natural ass tonight. Dey tearin' mah ole dickstring loose.

STEVE (*Fake concern*)

Hey . . . what'chou mathafukkers doin' ta Montgomery?

TOOTSIE (*Chortles*)

Maaan . . . I ain't doin' nothin' ta Montgomery . . . and wouldn't if'n I could. Everybody knows dat Montgomery's like a fatha ta me jest like he is to you, Stevie. Heee heee hee . . . he's just runnin' inta some baad luck tonight, dat's all. His real son over there . . . old Marc's tearin' the old man a brand-new one . . . whoweee . . .

MARCO (*Feigns agitation and flares nostrils*)

Gawd damn!

(*Indignation*)

If that ain't a bitch? This dickhead Tootsie Franklin has been settin' Montgomery all night and he blames it on me!

MONTGOMERY (*Laments*)

Gawd damn right . . . now ya mention it, son.

(*Points to* TOOTSIE)

This long drawn-out gigglin' fellah who goes for mah tall son has been settin' his ole play daddy all night.

(*Droll dialect*)

Wha don't cha lighten up on the ole man, baby boy?

(*Clutches his head and rolls his eyes*)

Aww . . . me . . . Tootsie. Whoe wooooooe is me, boy . . . don't do it ta da ole man like dat, son. Ohh ohh mah goddamned achin' arse!

(*The young men laugh throughout.*)

TOOTSIE (*Giggles*)
I ain't done nothin' ta ya, pop. It's dat Marco ov'va dere who's helpin' ta set ya.

MARCO (*Groans*)
Sheet . . . I'm losin' mah balls and you come with that shit about it's my fault he's gettin' set.

TOOTSIE (*Teases*)
Boy, you's a hard loser, Marc . . . hee hee hee . . . but, I'm sho glad he ain't settin' me all those times as he is you, Montgomery . . . heee heee . . . whew, dad. Your son's sho kickin' yo' ass.

MARCO
Aww . . . what a chickenshit game this is! Pinochle . . . penny-a-point, double-deck, cut-throat pinochle. Fifty cents a set. Five hundred to go out. Aww . . . with these two on each side of you . . . what a chickenshit game!

TOOTSIE
You ain't doin' so bad, Marc. I'm losin' so far.

MONTGOMERY
Damn right . . . you ain't been in the hole yet, baby boy.

MARCO

Deal!

TOOTSIE

How much meld you got, Marco?

MARCO

Not enough!

TOOTSIE (*Peers at laid-out hands*)

That's one hundred and eighty-three for Montgomery, twenty-eight for Marc . . .

MARCO

C'mon . . . deal the cards.

MONTGOMERY

You's a hard loser, son.

STEVE

How long you been playin'?

TOOTSIE

Since about eight—we just countin' our meld now. Stick around and you can get a hand in a few minutes, Steve.

(STEVE's *entrance gives the three players time to light cigarettes, scratch themselves and refill their glasses. On a nearby table a half gallon of white port stands and several cans of concentrated lemon juice. There are also a couple of half-emptied quarts of ale and three fourths of a pint of scotch.*

TOOTSIE *lifts his glass.*)

MARCO

Damn . . . how can you drink that fukkin' wine that fast, Tootsie Franklin?

(*Caught with a filled glass halfway to his lips,* TOOTSIE *peers over the rim, grins with braggadocio, shakes his head in satisfaction and gulps down half the contents.*)

TOOTSIE (*Gasps and shakes his head*)

Ahh . . . I drink it like it's water, dat's all.

MONTGOMERY

Gawd damn . . . boy! Don't that white port and lemon juice rot your liver, Tootsie?

TOOTSIE

Like water . . . same difference ta me. All you gotta do is take the glass . . .

(*Lifts glass and drains*)

and just drink it down.

(TOOTSIE *shudders as the mixture falls into his stomach, and wags his narrow head.*)

Maaan, dat sho is some good stuff.

MARCO/MONTGOMERY (*Together*)

Gawd damn!

(MARCO *gives a demonstration with an imaginary wine mug, lifting his arms, pulling back his head; his hat falls back and dangles by its cord around his neck; he gapes, then leans forward and brushes the invisible drool from his mouth.*)

MARCO

Glug, glug, glug glug! Ahh . . .

TOOTSIE

Guess I better go lightly now. Keep on drinkin' like dat an'
dere won't be none left fo' later.

MARCO (*To* STEVE)

Hey, poppa, get yourself a drink.

MONTGOMERY

Yeah, son, would you like some of this good scotch?

STEVE

Okay, thanks. In a minute.

> (*He walks into the kitchen and turns on the light.*
>
> *Downstairs,* VELMA *turns on her light and sits up
> in bed. She listens as* STEVE *opens the refrigerator
> and takes out a bottle of ale.*
>
> *The light goes off downstairs as he rejoins the card
> players.*)

TOOTSIE (*To* MARCO *and* MONTGOMERY)

Yeah, I know dey ain't mah kids, not all of dem anyways . . .
but dey might as well be mine.

MARCO (*Mocks*)

"Dey might as well be mine."

MONTGOMERY

How long you and Lola been broke up, Tootsie?

TOOTSIE

Three years. We ain't never been together 'cept'n fo' two months when we first got married. But her mother was livin' wit us den, so I got in a couple of hassles wit Lola and her mamma and then I split. I still go back and see her. We good friends.

MARCO (*Sighs*)

Yeah, you still do see her "Hanky-Panky" Franklin.

TOOTSIE (*Shrugs*)

It don't bother me none if'n she has dem kids an' blames dem on me. Kids need somebody fo' dere fatha . . . heee heee . . . and the welfare people downtown don't care who takes the blame. They don't even bother me too much. Whenever they git me I jest say I'm out ah work or claim bankruptcy . . .

MARCO (*Laughs*)

Claim bankruptcy!

MONTGOMERY

Son . . . I want to enlighten your young mind. . . . You were in bankruptcy when you were first born.

TOOTSIE (*Continues*)

. . . makes no never mind ta me.

MARCO

Hey, Franklin. Since everybody's fukkin' Lola, how about lettin' me get a little bit?

(*Three-beat pause*)

TOOTSIE (*Grins*)

Heee heee . . . everybody might be fukkin' her alright, and I don't mind none, ya understand, but I better not ev'va ketch you wit her.

(TOOTSIE'*s expression gradually changes; he is solemn, waggles his head slightly, nervously, and taps the tabletop with his long index finger.*)

MARCO (*Mock seriousness*)

Why, Franklin? I'm your buddy, ain't I, man? Why, I'd take better care of her than most any other ole nigger out there in the streets.

TOOTSIE (*Resolute and staring*)

Yeah, man, dat might be right, but you's also my friend, an' dat's not the same as somebody I don't know, so if I ev'va ketch ya with mah ole lady, I'm goin' ta kill ya.

(*Silence.*

Glasses are lifted and their contents gulped; chairs are scraped, throats cleared and feet shuffled.

MONTGOMERY *lifts a leg and with his lips makes an unpleasant noise.*)

MARCO (*Bellows*)

Gawd damn, paw!

TOOTSIE (*Laughs and pretends to gag*)

Wheweee . . . Montgomery . . . sometimes you's about as decent as a dawg.

Gawd damn! Somethin' must'a crawled up you and died, paw.

> (STEVE *walks into the dark kitchen and lifts a window;* TOOTSIE *goes to the backstairs and opens the door.*
>
> *Below,* VELMA *gets out of her bed and walks slowly through her darkened apartment to the backstairs.*)

MARCO

Hey, Mr. B, the landlady's been lookin' fo' ya since last night.

TOOTSIE

Some people have all the luck.

STEVE (*Sarcastic*)

Sho do.

TOOTSIE (*Shakes his head*)

But I sho wouldn't want to be in yo' shoes fo' anything, Stevie Benson.

MONTGOMERY (*Signifying*)

Ohhh . . .

MARCO (*Grins at* STEVE)

Yeah. When "Hamfists" gets a hold of our boy Stevie it's goin'a be just too bad.

> (STEVE *remains silent.*)

MONTGOMERY

"Hamfists?"

TOOTSIE (*Laughs*)

Yeah, O.K., her great big gorilla-lookin' husband.

(MARCO *and* TOOTSIE *giggle.*)

MARCO (*To* STEVE)

Where ya been, fartstick?

STEVE

Oh, I was down at a friend's, you know Len, don't ya?

MARCO

Len . . . Len? I don't think so. Wait, does he go to City College?

STEVE

Yeah.

MARCO

Hey, wait a minute . . . you don't mean a little short, stocky guy . . .

(*Singsong*)

wit mo' hair den yo' eyes can see?

STEVE

Yeah.

MARCO

Heee heee heee . . . hey, boy, I guess you's really been out. Woweee . . .

TOOTSIE (*Suspicious*)

Who's dis Len guy, Steve?

MARCO

Ahhh, he's just some beatnik kind'a guy we know at school. Right, Stevie?

MONTGOMERY

You messin' round with beatniks, son?

TOOTSIE

Heee heee heee . . . sounds like a woman wit all dat hair y'all talk about.

MARCO

Might sound like a woman but he ain't.

STEVE

Nawh . . . he's straight. Got a little sharp girl livin' with him.

(MONTGOMERY *weaves on his chair and shakes a finger in* STEVE's *face.*)

MONTGOMERY

I'm sure glad of that, sonny boy. Don't want ta hear of mah fat son fuggin' punks . . . Keep yo' dick out'ta dose fat round eyes, buddy boy. And dat goes fo' mah long lanky son too.

TOOTSIE (*Indignant*)

Montgomery, you couldn't melt me an' po' me on a punk!

MONTGOMERY (*Turns to* MARCO)

And mah sweet-lookin' son here, he better watch hisself or his ole daddy might stick him one when he's not lookin'.

(A chorus of laughs from STEVE *and* TOOTSIE*)*

MARCO *(Embarrassed)*

Fuck you . . . you ole reprobate . . . propositioning your own son.

MONTGOMERY *(Innocence)*

But, I wasn't, baby boy. I only was lettin' ya know what might be in store fo' ya so ya better sleep on yo' back from now on in, sweetie, and keep one eye cocked fo' the old man.

MARCO

I'll keep my blade cocked for your long skinny ass.

TOOTSIE *(Signifying)*

Now I don't want ta be gettin' inta yo' business, but . . .

(The group bursts out laughing and becomes choked and unable to speak.

VELMA *has climbed the backstairs and is standing in the kitchen outside the door to* MARCO's *room. She knocks and looks in the door. There is a toothsome grin on her face.)*

VELMA

Good evening, gentlemens. Would you mind if I drag Stevie Bentan away for a while?

MARCO *(Gracious)*

Why, not at all, landlady. Here . . . take ole shithead here.

(She giggles.)

TOOTSIE

Hi, Velma. How ya doin'?

VELMA (*Soft Southern accent*)

Why, just fine, Tootsie. How ya'all?

STEVE (*Stands*)

Say, Velma, have you met Marc's father, Montgomery?

VELMA

Why no, I haven't. How'd do?

MONTGOMERY

Why fine, sister. Hey, don't stand out there in the cold. Step on in here. Why, all mah ole eyes can see is your pretty head. These hare boys ain't gonna bite ya.

TOOTSIE

At least not before you do, paw.

MARCO

You better watch yourself around this ole man, Velma. He doesn't know he's as old as he is.

MONTGOMERY

Why, son, you shouldn't be sayin' those things about your lovin' daddy.

MARCO

Nawh . . . I take that back. You're too skinny, Velma . . . paw likes his girls to be at least two hundred pounds or more.

TOOTSIE (*Giggles*)

Woweee . . . dat's right. Montgomery does go fo' dem elephant and hippopotamus broads.

Well, Marco, I ain't exactly skinny . . . ask Steve. Stevie
. . . tell Mr. Montgomery that I ain't skinny.

MONTGOMERY

Wahl, come on in here, gal, and show me.

VELMA (*Moves more into the doorway*)

Well, I'd like to come in for a while but I ain't dressed fo'
it. And I see that Marc wasn't expectin' company either.

MONTGOMERY

Ain't dressed fo' it? Then why you allow mah lil' fat woman-
chasin' son out there with you, sister? I don't think you rightly
know what you're doin' if you one of them virtuous types.

VELMA (*Enjoying the attention*)

Oh, I know what I'm doin' alright. Ya see, Stevie's mah
friend. We understand one another . . . ya understand that?

MARCO

Hey, landlady . . . just 'cause I ain't got no clothes on ain't
no reason for you to stand out there.

MONTGOMERY

Yeah . . . I guess I am hip ta *that*, baby girl.

VELMA (*Smiles*)

Ahhh, go on, Mr. Montgomery. And, Marco, I ain't comin'
in dere with you just havin' yo' drawers on. C'mon, Steve.

MONTGOMERY

Call me Montgomery, gal. None of that mister stuff.

STEVE (*Leaves*)

See you guys in a few minutes.

MONTGOMERY

Call me Montgomery, Miss Landlady. Just Montgomery.

VELMA (*Exiting*)

Okay, Montgomery. Good night. Night, Marco . . . night, Tootsie.

> (*The two descend the backstairs as the light in* MARCO's *room lowers and the stair lights go up softly.*)

TOOTSIE

Ummm ummm . . . some people have all the luck.

MONTGOMERY (*Slapping his thigh*)

Hope ta gawd dey do!

MARCO

Deal!

TOOTSIE (*Giggles*)

But I still wouldn't want to be in his shoes for anything . . . if "Hamfists" . . .

MARCO

Go on 'n deal!

> (*Lights blacken upstairs.*)

SCENE 2

A soft spot shows STEVE *and* VELMA *sitting at the foot of the backstairs.*

The scene is played sensually; STEVE *attempts to arouse her through gestures and caresses.*

VELMA (*Angry*)

Where you been?

STEVE

If I told you, you wouldn't know.

VELMA

Wouldn't I? Well, I know already . . . you been out with some girl!

STEVE (*Deliberate*)
And if I were?

VELMA
You playin' me fo' a fool, Stevie!

(*He tries to put his arm about her; she pulls away.*)

STEVE
Look, Velma, don't give me a bad time, huh?

VELMA
You talk about me givin' you a bad time? What about me sittin' here waitin' fo' O.D. to come in an' beat mah ass or fo' you to drag in at two in the mornin' an' treat me like ah piece ah shit?

STEVE (*Starts to rise*)
I don't see where this is gettin' . . .

VELMA (*Cutting, pulls him back and warns*)
Don't do this ta me, Stevie!

STEVE (*Ridicules*)
Don't do what to you? I just walked in the door, remember?

VELMA
You walked in the door alright. You smart sonna bitch!

STEVE
Watch the names, Velma.

VELMA
You move in here an' find that I'm alone most of the time

and you start in actin' like a man until you get what you
want . . . then . . .

STEVE

I didn't rape you!

VELMA

You know I was lonely. I'm a married woman . . . you know
I wouldn't let you touch me after only three days unless I
was lonely and . . .

STEVE

Stop talkin' stupid!

VELMA (*Bitter*)

Think because the government's sendin' ya ta college . . .
you think that you wise. . . . Well, I got news fo' ya, Mr.
Stevie Bentan . . .

STEVE (*Tired*)

The name's Benson, Velma.

VELMA

It don't make no difference what it is . . . just means dirty
nigger ta me. They sendin' a lot ah stupid dirty niggers to
school fo' shootin' Koreans or North Vietnams or Red China-
men or whatever they is . . . and you black niggers won't
even act like men when you get home. . . . You should be
ashamed of yourself, nigger!

STEVE (*Sullen*)

Don't call me a nigger again.

VELMA (*Ignores his remark*)

Remember I helped put that mathafukkin' husband of mine, O.D., through auto mechanics school. I put his black ass through school. *Me* and the G.I. Bill! Haaa . . . some goddamn shit, man. He wasn't dumb enough ta stay out of the army but when he got out of there he got himself sent ta school . . . an' that fool's plumb crazy . . . don't know shit . . . so I know you and Marco must be goin' ta be professors, or sumpten.

STEVE (*Puts his arm about her*)

Listen, baby . . .

VELMA (*Continues*)

Since that first day two months ago you've had me up on your couch whenever you wanted and now you treat me like a tramp, when I ask you where you been after you stay out fo' two days. Remember I got a husband who's makin' ah ca-reerah ah stayin' out in the streets. Why shouldn't I ask you where you been? Because you playin' me fo' a sucker, man!

STEVE

No, I'm not! I just spent the weekend out with a friend. A guy I know from school. . . . I have another week of vacation from work, so I just thought I'd get out of the house for a while.

VELMA

But leavin' me home by myself. How 'bout if O.D. came in an' began beatin' on me?

STEVE

Listen, Velma, he's your husband . . . just because . . .

VELMA (*Furious*)

Don't say that! Don't tell me about my husband when he does what he does to me. You know how I looked when you first moved in?

STEVE

Awww . . . did he come?

VELMA

Well, how 'bout if he did?

STEVE

He didn't!

VELMA

You know you're the only reason he don't beat mah ass much anymo'. Since you come down an' stopped him that time. . . .

STEVE

That was an accident. . . . I was in the wrong place at the wrong time. I got no business tellin' him what ta do with his wife.

VELMA

Sheet . . . O.D.'s so bad on me he don't want anybody ta know how he is, an' he knows you'll come down from upstairs if you hear me hollarin' . . . he don't even come by much anymo'. He don't even think I'm doin' nothin' 'cept waitin' on him.

STEVE

So he won't bother you . . . but he's your husband, baby.

VELMA

Husband . . . haaa . . . not fo' two years has he been a husband to me.

STEVE

One of your kids is less than two years old.

VELMA

I don't mean that kind'a husband. . . . He'd like ta give me ah mathafukkin' baby every six months if he could. But I ain't gonna let him climb on me after he's been with his little bitch. He stays over cross town with that little black bitch of his. You know the only time he comes by here is to change his clothes and eat and then try and get me in bed.

STEVE

I'm not talkin' 'bout that, Velma. You're still married to him . . . he's got a good job, gives you money, sends money to take care of your kids in Tennessee and takes care of you pretty good.

VELMA

That mathafukker's just sorry fo' the way he treats me, that's all. And he'll be sorrier one day.

STEVE

You must love him a lot to be so bitter.

VELMA (*Not hearing*)

Always comin' in when he's drunk an' cryin' an' askin' me ta love him and that he's sorry. And before I know it he's got me down chokin' an' rapin' me. He's not in his right mind.

(*Evil*)

He'll really be sorry one day.

STEVE

Listen, baby, I don't want to argue with you.

(*He pulls her to him and kisses her. His hands move over her thin gown.*)

Now look at it from my point of view. I work part-time and get a very small check from the government for tryin' to finish school. You're married, baby, with a husband that doesn't seem to want to let you go, even if we could get together . . . and you got three small kids in Tennessee at your mother's . . . now . . .

VELMA

You just like the rest . . . you just wanted what you could get from me . . .

STEVE

It's been nice, Velma, and we can still be friends. . . . Now wasn't it nice between us?

VELMA (*Crying*)

You sonna bitch!

STEVE (*Wrings her arm*)

I told you not to curse me!

VELMA

Go on, break it! Do anything you want. I got one mathafukker who gets his nuts off ah beatin' mah ass . . . another one don't matter!

(*She cries and looks defiant.*)

STEVE (*Soothes*)

Nawh . . . it's not like that, Velma. I really like you, you understand, but I've got a future and you seem to have yours cut out for you . . .

VELMA (*Bitter*)

What kinda future did you have when I met you, huh? I fed you for six weeks until your check came. I let your rent go for a month until you found a job which *suited* your school schedule. I gave you the money for your tuition and books!

STEVE (*Kisses her*)

Velma, baby . . .

VELMA (*Resolute*)

He'll kill me . . . one day O.D. will kill me!

STEVE

Oh, Velma . . .

VELMA (*Exhausted*)

He can't let me go and he can't keep me around. I should'a known better than to let him talk me into leavin' the kids down home with my parents.

STEVE

Why don't you go back home? You got some money saved.

VELMA

He told me it was so we could get on our feet better. . . . We should come out west and work so we could save more money to buy a house. Well, I saved some, as much as I could, but he took it! So I saved more by myself, and he's mad at me

'cause I won't give it to him . . . for that little black bitch
of his!

STEVE

You got folks back there. You could sit down and think it
all out.

VELMA

He makes almost two hundred fifty a week with overtime but
after he takes care of the lease here and that bitch's rent
cross town the rest is just enough fo' him and her to get
drunk on every night and fo' him always actin' like a fool.

STEVE

He gives you almost a hundred bucks a week.

VELMA

If I didn't rent out the upstairs he would have me just where
he wants.

STEVE

Where does he want you, Velma?

(*He caresses her more.*)

VELMA

Steve . . . ?

STEVE

Yeah.

VELMA

Be mah friend . . . please be mah friend.

STEVE (*Pulls her to him*)
Sure, baby . . . I'm your . . .

VELMA (*Pushes him back*)
Not just like that!

STEVE (*Piqued*)
Well, what do you want, Velma? What can I do?

(*She stands and stares down at him, then she turns
and exits, going to her bedroom.*

Spot down; upstairs, lights up on the card players)

SCENE 3

TOOTSIE

Oeeweee . . . I don't know how I pulled that out of the fire.

MARCO

You lucky fuck.

MONTGOMERY

Damn, you the luckiest, Franklin.

MARCO

You ain't got nothin' ta complain about, paw.

TOOTSIE

Lucky? Shit, I just played it dat way. Look'a hare!

(*He displays the score sheet which he keeps with an accountant's accuracy.*)

One time I was sev-van-tee-ate in da hole. Owweee . . . I sho had ta come a long ways.

STEVE (*Enters*)
Hey, Stevie Benson, ya want ta play partners this game?

STEVE
Okay, I guess I'll play one. Penny-a-point, right? Fifty cents a set? Who's my partner?

MARCO
Me, fartstick.

(*They arrange themselves around the table.*)

Before we start I think we should take a little break.

(*He slips his hat off and turns it over. From under the sweatband he takes a small, brown cigarette. He hands it to* STEVE.)

I want you to try some of this shit.

(*The music plays low.*)

STEVE
Thanks, man.

(*He picks open the capped end and wets it with his tongue and lips. When he lights it, the first puff chokes him, and he looks ashamed and hands it to* TOOTSIE.)

TOOTSIE
Nawh, forget me. Dose things don't do nothin' fo' me. Just be wastin' yo' good weed on me.

MONTGOMERY (*Interested*)

Yeah? That's too bad, sonny boy. I ain't never had any of that . . . let me try some of that stuff, Stevie.

(*The cigarette is passed around, and* STEVE *and* MARCO *look at* TOOTSIE *and giggle.*)

TOOTSIE

What'cha lookin' at me fo'? Is dat what dat stuff does ta ya? Makes ya act like ah little gigglin' girl?

(*It passes again to* TOOTSIE.)

Maaan, dat marijuana stuff don't do nothin' ta me . . . hummp . . . but, okay, if ya wants ta waste it.

(*He takes several extraordinary drags, showing by the expansion of his narrow chest how deeply he inhales. He passes it around, coughs slightly.*)

Think I'll have another taste of dat wine.

STEVE (*Laughs*)

Wine . . . wine . . . spo dee oodee . . . wine . . . hee hee . . . in de wine times . . . yeah . . .

TOOTSIE (*Eyes glistening; simpering*)

What'cho say, Stevie? Do you want some mo' of dis white port and lemon juice?

STEVE

I ain't had none of that stuff, man.

TOOTSIE

Heee heee . . . maan, dis is a funny drink.

MARCO

What'cha laughin' at, "Hanky-Panky" Franklin?

MONTGOMERY

Heee heee . . . what you call Franklin "Hanky-Panky" for,
son? Ha ha ha . . . "Hanky-Panky" Franklin . . .

MARCO (*Slyly*)

What's so funny, pawh?

MONTGOMERY (*Loudly, but to himself*)

Gawd damn . . . if dat ain't da stone goddamned truth. . . .
Dere is somethin' in dat after all . . . heee heee heeee . . .
sheet.

(*He props his head in his hands.*)

TOOTSIE

Heee heee heee . . .

STEVE (*Mumbles*)

I said the wine . . . you know. . . . Oh, yeah, po' me ah
little ah dat stuff, won't chou please?

(*Silence and intermittent giggles.* MAMMA's *voice
comes from next door.*)

MAMMA (*Off; shouting*)

Hey, ov'va dere . . . what'cha doin' . . . what'cha bein' so
quiet!

(*All are immediately alert*)

MONTGOMERY (*Frightened*)

Gawd damn . . . what's that?

36

TOOTSIE
Is dis what dat stuff does ta ya, man?

MAMMA (*Top of voice*)
I know ya ov'va dere playin' cards an' drinkin' an' cussin' like the rascals ya are. . . . I see yo' lights an' I could hear ya dirty talk ah few minutes ago. . . . What's cha doin'? It ain't right fo' ya ta be so quiet! What'cha doin'? Hey, Marco . . . Marco. . . . Hey, Marco!

(VELMA *turns her light on downstairs but remains in bed, listening.*

The quieter voice of POPS *is heard.*)

POPS (*Off; appealing*)
It's three o'clock in the mornin', Mamma. Those boys ov'va dere are mindin' dere own business.

STEVE (*To* MONTGOMERY *and* TOOTSIE)
Ohhh . . . Jesus . . . it's drunken Mamma from nex' door stoned out of her mind. . . . She's on one of her early mornin' rampages.

MAMMA (*To* POPS)
But dey all ov'va dere with Velma . . . an' she's by herself wit' all them ole dirty mouf, piss-ass men and boys.

(MARCO *has walked to the window of the kitchen.*)

MARCO (*Shouts*)
Shut up, Mamma! Can't ah goddamn soul get some peace and quiet around hare?

MAMMA (*Off; at the top of her voice*)

Marco, is dat you! Hey, cousin, why you so quiet?

MARCO

Don't come with that cousin crap, Mamma. I'd blow my brains out if I had somebody like you in my family!

POPS (*To* MARCO, *not as loud as the others*)

Marco, Mamma just wanted to know if all of you were all right.

MARCO

It's quiet over here 'cause I'm gettin' me a little bit, Mamma. Now you and Pops get you ah little some if ya still can!

MAMMA

Ya ah filthy mouf puppy, Marco!

MARCO

Go on back ta ya drinkin' an' mind ya business!

POPS (*Off; to* MAMMA)

See, Mamma, I told ya. See, dere ain't nothin' ta worry 'bout!

MAMMA (*Suspicious*)

Marco, ya sure ain't nothin' goin' on ov'va dere?

MARCO

Yeah, Mamma, I'm sure. We just takin' some dope an' lookin' at dirty pictures, that's all!

MAMMA

I still don't see or hear Stevie . . . ain't he home yet? And where's Velma? Is O.D. dere?

(*Dogs bark.*)

Velma . . . hey, Velma . . . Velma . . . Hey, Velma . . .

(*Downstairs,* VELMA *switches her light off.*

SISTER SUKIE'*s voice comes from the other side of the duplex.*)

SISTER SUKIE (*Shouts*)
Hey, what's goin' on? Mamma? Marco?

STEVE (*Rises and walks to window*)
Hey, that sounds like Sister Sukie.

TOOTSIE (*Follows him*)
Sister Sukie?

STEVE (*Calls out the window*)
Hi, Mamma. Hi, Pops.

SUKIE
Hey, what's all the shoutin' 'bout?

MARCO
Sukie, go on back to sleep . . . it ain't nothin'!

MAMMA
Why, hi dere, Stevie. How ya doin', son?

SUKIE (*Indignant*)
Marco Polo Henderson, don't you tell me when to go back to sleep. What do you mean there's nothin' goin' on round here?

MARCO

If you keep hollarin' like that, Miss Sukie . . . I'm goin'
ta come ov'va there and get me a little bit from your fat
booty!

SUKIE

Oooeee, Marco . . . I didn't know you were so fresh, boy.
I'm goin' ta come ov'va your house tomorrow and give you a
piece of mah mind.

MARCO

You goin' ta give me a piece, Sukie Mae, but it ain't goin'
ta be from around your mind!

SUKIE

Oooooooooo . . . Marco . . .

STEVE

Hey, Mamma, do you know Tootsie here?

MAMMA

Yeah . . . I've seen that ole long lanky boy before.

TOOTSIE

Hey, do you folks do this every night?

MAMMA

Nawh, son, we usually take off Sundays. Hey, you boys seen
Velma?

MARCO

Yeah . . . a little bit earlier. . . . She's sleepin' now . . .
come on over tomorrow and see her.

POPS

Yeah, Mamma, we can see Velma tomorrow.

MAMMA

Okay, you boys. I'm goin' now . . . see you in the mornin'.

(*Only several dogs bark occasionally.*

Lights go down in MARCO's *room as the three young men join* MONTGOMERY *at the table.*
Spot on ringing telephone downstairs, in the BESTS' *living room.*)

VELMA (*Answers*)

Yeah, Mamma, what is it now!

MAMMA (*Off*)

Velma, honey, how did you know it was me? Is you alright, girl?

VELMA (*Peeved*)

Yeah, I'm okay, Mamma. Woman . . . you worst than my own mamma back in Tennessee.

MAMMA

Well . . . I only wanted to know if you was alright.

POPS (*Off*)

What she say?

VELMA

Yeah . . . I'm just great, Mamma. Just need some sleep, dat's all.

POPS

What she say, Mamma?

MAMMA (*To* POPS)

Hush up, man.

VELMA

Now give my best to Pops, Mamma. Now, good night.

MAMMA

Good night, Velma . . . Velma?

VELMA

Yeah?

MAMMA

O.D. ain't been around, has he?

VELMA

Nawh . . . that sonna bitch is somewheres gettin' his good rest tonight. But he'll be 'round here hell raisin' in the mornin', I 'spect. So, good night, Mamma.

(*She hangs up. Spot off; lights up in* MARCO's *room*)

SCENE 4

The card game.

TOOTSIE (*Throws in his hand*)
Wow, dat sho was the funniest game I ev'va played. This marijuana stuff makes you see funny, man.

MARCO
Shit, shit shit shit SHIT.

MONTGOMERY
Son, you sure are a bad loser.

MARCO (*Appeals to* STEVE)
Bad loser! With the luck of you two lucky fucks! Tootsie Franklin . . . and Montgomery Saltsprings Henderson. Gawd damn! Have ya ever seen anything like it?

STEVE (*Rises*)

Well, I better get a couple of hours' sleep. It's been a hard weekend and if I don't get some sleep I won't be able to study tonight. It's Sunday already. Hey, what time is it?

MONTGOMERY

It's almost five, Stevie.

(STEVE *lifts a quart of ale from the side table and drinks from it.*)

TOOTSIE (*Yawns*)

I ain't had no sleep fo' days.

MARCO (*Needles*)

You ain't, Tootsie Franklin?

TOOTSIE (*Grins sheepishly*)

No, man, I ain't had no sleep fo' three days. . . . Heee heee 'cept'n las' night.

MARCO

Gawd damn! What a liar!

TOOTSIE (*Smirks*)

No, man, you can't even count dat. Shit, I really ain't slept fo' four days.

MARCO (*Mimics*)

"Cept'n las' night."

(*Disgust*)

Jeezus!

MONTGOMERY

(*Stands and takes the bottle from* STEVE)

Well, well, well, goddamn if it ain't that time fo' me too, sonny boy. Thanks for the relaxation . . . and . . .

(*Speaks to* MARCO *and winks*)

hey there, baby boy. Whenever ya got any mo' of them thar hat tricks just let the ole man know.

(MARCO *tosses his cards to slide and spread over the table.*)

MARCO (*Shouts*)

Hey, let's play one more!

(TOOTSIE *blinks groggy eyes and shakes his body like a puppy.*)

TOOTSIE

Okay by me. Heee heee . . . you's the ones who's gotta be studying tomorrow.

STEVE (*Frowns*)

Forget about it.

MARCO (*Excited*)

Okay, that makes Tootsie and me and paw. You playin', ain't you, paw?

MONTGOMERY

Sonny boy? Ya wants ya daddy ta screw ya some more?

(STEVE *exits.*)

TOOTSIE (*Dealing*)

Ya know I really do like skinny lil' boney girls. Montgomery
. . . I don't see how ya can stand dose big fat elephant
broads.

MONTGOMERY (*Counseling*)

Son . . . let me tell ya . . .

(*Lights down on card players.*

STEVE *walks through his room and enters bathroom.
Light shows around door; sound of water from
faucet. From the foot of the stairs,* VELMA'S *voice*)

VELMA (*Near whisper*)

Stevie? Is that you, Stevie?

(*The faucet is turned off. Bathroom door opens;
shirtless,* STEVE *is framed in the doorway.*)

STEVE

Yeah. Wait a minute.

(*Leaving the bathroom door opened, he descends
the stairs. Stops before her.*

Silence.

The light from the bathroom gives dim illumination.

*He puts his hands under her armpits, pulls her to
him and kisses her. She jerks her head back.*)

VELMA

You playin' me fo' a fool, Steve!

STEVE

Let's go up to my place.

VELMA

Nawh, not tonight. I can't hear if O.D.'s car drives up or if the telephone rings . . .

(He pulls her about and pushes against her bedroom door; she resists.)

STEVE *(Growls)*

C'mon!

VELMA *(Determined)*

No! I can't do that!

STEVE *(Piqued)*

What's the matter with you!

VELMA

I just can't . . . in there . . . it's my marriage bed.

STEVE

What!

VELMA

Please try an' understand.

(Silence.

Then he pulls her to him, kisses her as their shadowy forms ease to the floor.

Lights down.

Silence.

Lights up in bathroom, showing TOOTSIE *and* MONT-GOMERY *framed in doorway on their way downstairs.*)

TOOTSIE

Jeezus, Montgomery, how did we get sucker'd in'ta dat? I was three dollahs ahead an' Marc was losin' . . .

MONTGOMERY (*Wryly*)

That'll jest show ya how ya young'uns fuck the ole man.

TOOTSIE

Awww, Montgomery, you still won somethin'; it was Stevie who got in an' dropped his bread. He saved both of y'all.

(*They reach the foot of the staircase.*

Yells)

Goddamn! Wha . . . the hell! Heee Heeeeee ho ho . . .

(TOOTSIE *roars in the dim hallway, before stumbling offstage, gasping for more laughs.*)

MONTGOMERY (*Debonair*)

Wahl . . . I see mah lil' fat son is got enough sense not ta waste his nights.

(*He exits.*

Silence)

VELMA (*Whimpering*)
You *gotta* be mah man, now, Stevie. Now you gotta!

STEVE
Yeah, I know, baby. I know.

(*Lights down*)

CURTAIN

Second Movement

PARTY KILLER

the way we jerk in the dark
party killer
the mug of warm dago red
killer/diller
the red naked bulb
he's a chiller
the water of the toilet
empties behind the door
party killer
a cough
wheeler/dealer
your smell
he's a thriller
the stiff scrape of a
starched shirt

party killer
your breath
party killer
the final flame of a candle's flame
party killer
your kiss
killer/diller
your hardness pushes against my skirt
he's a chiller
a whisper
party killer
a record falls upon the ears
wheeler/dealer
blues, baby
he's a thriller
iiimmmmmmmmm
baby
party killer
party time
pass me a Miller's
party killer
it's a monster
oooooeeeeeeeeeewwwwwwwwwww

SCENE 1

An early afternoon light shows into the duplex.

O.D. BEST *and* CROOK *stand in front of the door to the* BEST *apartment.*

O.D. *kicks the door in, breaking off its lock, and enters the bedroom.*

VELMA (*Bolts up in bed*)
O.D.! Man, what's wrong with you!

(*Upstairs,* MARCO *sits upright in his bed, and* STEVE *swings his legs to the floor and sits upon his couch, listening.*

Crouches on her knees upon the bed.)

53

O.D., ANSWER ME! WHY'D YOU BREAK IN THE
DOOR? YOU GOT'TA KEY!

> (O.D. *begins pulling out drawers, pulling their con-
> tents out, and lifts objects from the dresser, looking
> for something.*
>
> CROOK *saunters in, smirking. He is wiry and has
> his hair processed.*
>
> *To* CROOK)

What's wrong with your friend, Crook? Can't he talk? He's
gone crazy or somethin'?

CROOK

Sheet . . . how would ah know, Velma? He's your ole man,
not mine. Don't ask me.

> (MARCO *lays back in bed and covers his head with his
> pillow.*
>
> STEVE *has begun to dress.*)

VELMA

No, O.D., don't do that!

> (O.D. *has found her purse in the closet and is looking
> through it. She jumps from the bed and rushes him;
> he puts his big hand in her face and shoves her back
> across the bed.*)

STEVIE! STEVIE!

> (*Money is taken from the purse and the purse is
> thrown at her head as she ducks.*)

O.D. (*Saunters out, to* CROOK)
C'mon, man. Let's make it!

(*He leads the way into the hallway.*)

VELMA (*Cries, leans across her bed*)
You sonna bitch! You dirty black sonna bitch! Don't take
my money and give it to that whore!

(STEVE *comes running down the stairs; seeing the
two men he stops halfway.*)

CROOK (*Faces* STEVE, *to* O.D.)
Who's dis little sucker? A marine . . . or sumpten?

(*He steps toward* STEVE;

O.D. *comes back and touches* CROOK'*s shoulder.*

STEVE *stands still and watches the pair.*)

O.D. (*Stares up at* STEVE; *sneers*)
C'mon, Crook . . . it's only the guy from upstairs.

(*They exit.*

STEVE *goes to the bedroom door and looks at* VELMA
crying on the bed.)

MAMMA (*Off*)
O.D.! O.D.! Wait . . . I want ta talk ta ya! O.D.!

(*The sound of a car leaving*)

VELMA (*Lifts her head, screams*)
That black sonna bitch . . . he took my money! Took my
money . . . that black mathafukker!

(MAMMA *rushes in; she is a small, thin woman with disheveled hair, drooping dress and slapping slippers.*)

MAMMA (*Goes to* VELMA)
Awww . . . Velma . . . Velma, don't cry . . .

(*Hovers over her*)

Everything's gonna be alright, girl, don't cry none . . .

(POPS *comes in and brushes past* STEVE *as he starts back up the stairs.*)

POPS
S'cuse me, Stevie.

(STEVE *doesn't look around.*
Enters bedroom.)

Ahhh . . . what's the matter, Velma?

VELMA (*Crying*)
He took my money . . . all the money for the rent . . . he took it.

(*In his room,* STEVE *sits in a chair, looking pensively out front, as if he is at a window, his eyes fixed on the horizon.*)

MAMMA (*Slightly drunk*)
That . . . that damn O.D.

POPS
Mamma . . . maybe we should take her over our house . . . maybe we should take her over our house, Mamma.

MAMMA (*Bends over* VELMA)

Velma, I want you to come over my place for a while. C'mon with Pops and me.

(SISTER SUKIE *enters; she wears a robe, under it a nightgown, and she has on slippers.*)

SUKIE

Mamma! What's wrong with Velma?

POPS

O.D.'s been here and took her rent money.

SUKIE

Uummm uummm . . . time I hear that yellin' an' cryin' an' other racket . . . I know'd it was him 'round here cuttin' up!

(*She is a plump, pretty girl.*)

MAMMA (*Helps* VELMA *off the bed*)

Just lean on me, Velma . . . everythin's gonna be alright.

SUKIE

I would'a been here sooner but all that yellin' everybody was doin' las' night sounded just like this mess so I didn't think too much about it, at first.

MAMMA

You could'a come sooner if ya wanted, girl.

(*They lead* VELMA *out the door;* POPS *brings up the rear.*)

SUKIE

Now, Mamma, you know if I'd knew O.D. was around I'd been sittin' up here . . . 'cause he don't do nothin' ta her when I'm here . . .

> (*The party nearly collides with* WANDA *and* MARIE HORTON.
> *The two women wear high heels and dressy dresses.*)

MARIE (*Steps upon* POP'S *foot*)

Well, excuse me.

WANDA (*Shyly*)

Hi . . .

> (*The group ignores them except for* POPS *who hops away; they exit.*)

WANDA (*Puzzled*)

Wow!

MARIE

Goddamn, Wandie . . . What kinda joint have you brought me to? No sooner then we get here than they carrying out bodies.

WANDA (*Climbs stairs*)

I don't know, Aunt Marie . . . I hope they didn't come from Marco's place.

MARIE

Not unless he lives back there where that door's hangin' on its hinges.

(They stop at top of stairs and WANDA *knocks at* STEVE's *door.*

STEVE *answers knock as the lights blacken.*)

*STEVE, MARCO, WANDA and MARIE HORTON sit around
the table in MARCO's room. A large green bottle of
scotch sits upon the table. STEVE and MARCO have
ale cans in their hands. Jazz plays softly upon the
radio. MARCO is dressed in Levis and sports shirt.*

MARCO (*Languid and happy*)
Hey . . . hey . . . little Wanda and her swingin' aunt . . .
Aunt Marie . . . How y'all, Aunt Marie?

MARIE (*Kids*)
You sho are a crazy young nigger, boy. . . . No wonder
Wandie's so crazy for you . . . she's about as dumb as you
are . . .

WANDA
Awww . . . Aunt Marie . . .

(MARIE *is a heavy-set but good-looking matron in her mid-forties.*)

MARIE (*Annoyed, but joking*)
Woman . . . stop callin' me your fukken aunt with all these young men around here!

(MARCO *lets out a great laugh.*)

MARCO
HEE HAWWW . . . you call ole shithead Stevie Benson sittin' over there good-lookin'? Heee heee . . . heee heee. . . . Aunt Marie, honey, you need glasses.

MARIE (*To* STEVE)
You gonna let this little curly-headed cocksucker talk to you like that, sweetcake?

WANDA
Awww . . . stop teasin' Stevie, he's nice and besides I know somebody who likes him.

MARCO
Ole shithead here? Heee heee . . . they like him alright . . . they'd like him to get his assbone broke. . . . Ha ha . . . that's how much they like him awlright.

MARIE (*Laughs and is curious*)
Now I just met this young man, but he's too good-lookin' and intelligent a specimen for that. At least he looks like it . . . there ain't nothin' wrong with him that I can't see, is there?

STEVE
Yeah . . . there is . . . I got a wart in a strategic place.

MARIE (*Whoops*)

See, Wandie . . . see . . . I told you that you've brought me to the right place.

WANDA

Awww . . . you told me at first I hadn't . . . maybe I have, but Uncle Bob wouldn't think so.

MARIE

Sheet . . . your Uncle Bob is out kickin' up his legs in the bars . . . ha ha ha . . . and Miss Marie is out to do some leg kickin' herself, honey . . .

(*Laughs and snaps her fingers*)

just watch the old girl tonight . . . 'cause it's party time.

WANDA

You keep on drinkin' that scotch like that and you won't even know when the party starts.

MARCO

Bob might be out in the bars and not carin' much where you are but if you were Tootsie Franklin's ole lady . . . you'd always be wonderin' when the roof would fall in . . .

WANDA

Tootsie Franklin? Ahhh . . . how is Franklin?

MARCO (*Singsong*)

He's just as fine as wine. "Hanky-Panky" Franklin is fukken "A" ah rooney . . . yes, mam, lawdy . . . heee heee heee . . . yes, indeedy . . . heee ha ha . . .

He won most of the money last night.

Shit, will that nigger be around today?

MARCO

Heee heee . . . one time Franklin . . . heee heee . . . his
ole lady, Lola, some broad and me went to a dance at the
Southside Inn. Maaan, we was just drinkin' an' clownin' and
some guy came over who knew Lola, Franklin's ole lady.
Heee hee heeee . . . yeah, the dude just sat down without
askin' anybody . . . heee heee heee . . . and started in
talkin' to Lola and began sayin', "C'mon, baby, c'mon! Why
don't you come on home with me tonight. Let's split from
this square scene. C'mon, baby . . . awww . . . c'mon, you
remember the *last* time and how good it was?" HEEE HEEE
. . . yeah, that cat was talkin' right in front of Franklin,
real loud . . .

WANDA

Poor Franklin.

(*Below,* TOOTSIE FRANKLIN *enters and begins climbing the stairs.*)

MARCO

Yeah . . . this guy kept on "C'mon, Lola, baby. Awww,
c'mon, baby." And Franklin didn't say a word, just shook his
head like he does when somethin' bothers him and kept on
drinkin'. All that Lola said to the cat was: "Nawh . . . hee
hee . . . I can't . . . hee hee . . . please stop." And the
cat kept it up. Well, finally, we got ready to leave and then
that cat started really workin' on Lola . . . he began kissin'

her and tellin' her to come with him and then he said as we were puttin' on our coats, "Awww, *shit*, Lola, why don't you come with me, girl? *Damn!*" And Franklin knocked the shit out of the cat. Knocked his front teeth all over the lobby.

STEVE

He should have walked in his ass.

WANDA

Ohhh . . . I'm glad I wasn't there.

MARIE

Good thing you wasn't, Wandie. A silly little bitch like you would probably gone off with the mathafukker from the first and left your husband sittin' there.

WANDA

Aunt Marie . . . I mean, Marie . . . you know I'm not . . .

MARCO

But listen to this . . . heee heee ha ha ha . . . oh, Jesus! Franklin said after he hit the cat, "I don't let nobody cuss in front of mah wife!" Heee heee . . . hee heee . . . ha ha . . .

MARIE

Tootsie Franklin? You must be lyin', Marc. I bet there ain't no damn Tootsie Franklin.

MARCO

If you was the cat who had his gums busted and told about cussin' in front of his ole lady you'd know as much as you'd want to about Tootsie.

(TOOTSIE *enters*)

TOOTSIE

Who's usin' mah name in vain?

MARCO

Hey, hey . . . "Hanky-Panky" Franklin is on de scene.

WANDA

Marco, stop usin' all that bad talk. You know his name's not Hanky-Panky.

(TOOTSIE *wears a brightly colored shirt with ruffled lace down the front and at the sleeves. He also sports a red vest and charcoal, gray striped trousers.*

He points at STEVE *and giggles.*)

TOOTSIE

Stevie Benson . . . mah ole partner . . . the night rider.

STEVE

Fuck you, Franklin.

MARIE

This is Tootsie Franklin?

TOOTSIE (*Snappy, emphatic*)

Yes, mam!

(MARCO *whoops with laughter;* WANDA *giggles.*)

STEVE

Hey, Tootsie, you look like a Mississippi gambler.

WANDA

Awww . . . he looks nice.

STEVE

Well, I didn't say he didn't.

TOOTSIE

Wahl, I just put on dese hare clothes 'cause it's Sunday, ya know, ta dress up kinda, ya understand.

MARIE (*Shakes head and giggles*)

Now I believe everything.

MARCO

Hey, Franklin, this is Wanda's aunt, Marie.

MARIE (*Jokes*)

Don't tell people I'm that woman's aunt! Damn . . . she looks older than me.

WANDA (*Surprise*)

Aunt Marie . . .

(*Claps hand over mouth*)

Awww . . . Marie . . . you know I don't look older than you.

MARIE

Girl, you look bad as forty miles of dirt road.

(MARIE *grins. Waggling his head,* TOOTSIE *leans over the table slightly and concentrates upon the scotch.*)

TOOTSIE

Hello, Aunt Marie . . . what you doin' up here in dese hare boys' apartment?

MARIE (*Smiles widely*)

Why, young man, it's nice that you ask but it ain't to let you swill up my good scotch.

TOOTSIE

Why should you think that. I was just concerned about you keepin' your ladylike qualities, dat's all.

MARCO

Yeah, run it on down to her, Franklin. Heee heee hee . . .

MARIE (*Pours herself a drink*)

This is fo' me . . . 'cause this chippy's goin' ta party today.

(*She begins snapping her fingers, winking, and shaking her hips to the music.*)

WANDA

Tomorrow don't say I didn't warn you, Marie.

(**TOOTSIE** *pulls out a bottle hidden within his vest.*)

TOOTSIE

Well, I came prepared, myself.

STEVE

Oh, Jesus, Thunderbird wine.

MARCO

Go on in Stevie's room and grab a chair, Hanky-Panky.

TOOTSIE (*Begins to dance*)

I would if I could but I can't help mahself when the feeling comes down on me . . . owwweeee . . . yes, indeed . . .

MARIE (*Snaps fingers*)

Go on, Tootsie Franklin. Showboat, baby . . . floorshow!

(*They laugh as* TOOTSIE *dances, his tall slim form throwing shadows against the wall lit by a late afternoon sunlight.*)

MARCO (*Giggles*)

Go head, buggah head!

(SUKIE *enters downstairs and climbs the backstairs. She is dressed in tight-fitting slacks and jersey.*)

TOOTSIE (*Dances*)

Dis is called the "Backbone Puller."

(*His spectators laugh and drink as he shows them his improvised steps.*)

. . . and dis is tha "Funky Hunky" step. . . .

(*Seeing* SUKIE *as she reaches the top of the stairs*)

Hey, young lady! C'mon in here and dance wit me!

SUKIE (*Enters*)

Hi, everybody!

MARCO

Miss Sukie, baby! Did you come over to give me what you said you would today?

SUKIE (*Embarrassed*)

You better stop talkin' like that, Marco. You know I didn't
say nothin' like that.

STEVE

Like what, sweetie?

MARIE (*Grins, to* WANDA)

Wandie . . . looks like you got some competition.

WANDA

Awww . . . Aunt . . . I mean, Marie . . . stop teasin' me.

TOOTSIE (*Dancing*)

Hey, girl . . . hey Miss Sukie Mae . . . c'mon and dance
with me.

SUKIE

Nawh, I don't want ta dance, man. And how do you know
my name? I just heard all dis racket and came up.

MARCO

Gawd damn it, Sukie Mae. Get out there and dance!

SUKIE

Don't you talk to me like that, Marco! Who the hell . . .

STEVE (*Gently pushes her into* TOOTSIE)

Go on and play pretty, little mamma. Go on and dance
while I fix you a drink.

(MARCO *and* MARIE *laugh uproariously at* STEVE's
seductive tone.

TOOTSIE *and* SUKIE *dance expertly together as* VELMA *and* MAMMA *enter downstairs.*

Lights go down slowly upstairs though the music rises slightly and the dancers are seen in silhouette, as early evening light radiates through the windows.)

MAMMA

They havin' a party upstairs, Velma. You gonna stand fo' that?

VELMA

Yeah, Mamma. Somebody round here deserves to have some fun.

MAMMA

I bet they drinkin' and everything up there.

VELMA

Yeah, Mamma. You better get on up there before they drink it all up.

MAMMA

You think you gonna be alright now, Velma?

VELMA

Yeah, Mamma. I'm just gonna clean myself up before I get dressed fo' the party.

MAMMA

You gonna go . . . ?

VELMA

Yeah, I am!

MAMMA

Well, I guess I better go too . . . never tell what . . .

VELMA (*Sarcastic*)

Thanks, Mamma . . .

MAMMA

Them sure is some nice boys . . . not like . . .

VELMA (*Cutting*)

Don't talk about him! Don't talk about mah husband!

MAMMA

Ahhh . . . I'm sorry . . . I didn't . . .

VELMA

I have ta dress, Mamma . . .

(MAMMA *nods and turns; she goes out on the front porch and looks toward her house.*)

MAMMA

Hey, Pops! Hey, Pops! Come on ov'va! Come on ov'va, Pops!

(*She turns to climb the stairs but hesitates and calls once more.*)

Hey, you old-timey mathafukker . . . get yo' ass ov'va here . . . there's a party upstairs . . . ya hare me, man? Get on ov'va here, ya ole mathafukker!

(*Lights down*)

SCENE 3

Lights up, revealing the party scene.

During this scene there is continuous activity upon stage. MAMMA *and* POPS *stagger aimlessly and drunkenly about. Some of the younger people dance together or alone, beginning and stopping as they feel the music or their moods change. Conversations go on continually, overlapping, though some become the focus of the action. When this occurs lights dim in other areas of the stage and spots or special lighting pick out the speakers.*

The scene begins with the celebrants sitting, dancing and shuffling between the two upstairs rooms of the duplex.

Bottles of beer, wine and liquor sit on tables and other furniture. Glasses are in the hands of almost everyone.

A Ray Charles album plays softly throughout the scene.

MARCO (*To* WANDA)

Heee heee . . . yeah, Tootsie Franklin is the craziest nigger you ever want ta meet. We were workin' at the post office . . . ha ha ha. . . . Boy! Were we workin'!

WANDA

Awww . . . stop teasin' Tootsie Franklin, Marco.

MARIE

Keep quiet, Wandie. Let me hear . . .

MARCO

Tootsie would work from sunset until the sun rose again in the mornin'.

WANDA

Stop lyin', Marc.

MARCO

But that's the truth!

MARIE (*To* WANDA)

Shut up, heifer!

MARCO

Sometimes he'd work around the clock. . . . Gawd! The hours that nigger put in . . .

TOOTSIE (*Dances with* SUKIE)

What kinda funny style perfume you got on?

SUKIE

That's mah man killer.

MARCO

. . . twelve . . . sixteen hours. . . . Sometimes he'd work two days straight. He us'ta work *so* hard. And he wasn't bullshittin' like the rest of us . . . Tootsie Franklin was workin' his natural ass off, you can believe that! Yeah, we'd go off in back somewheres and eat and go to sleep or get loaded, but Franklin would be steady jammin' . . .

MAMMA (*Walks up to* TOOTSIE *and* SUKIE)

Did I hear somebody say somethin' about killin' a man?

STEVE (*To* TOOTSIE *in passing*)

Hey, why don't you let me have this dance with Sukie?

(STEVE *takes* SUKIE's *hand from around* TOOTSIE's *shoulder.* TOOTSIE *holds her about the waist.*)

(*Three-beat pause*)

TOOTSIE

Now that you've shook her hand what more do you want?

(STEVE *and* TOOTSIE *look at each other.*)

MARCO

We got so we was callin' Tootsie Franklin "Mad Dawg" down on the job.

MARIE

"Mad Dawg?"

MARCO

Yeah, baby, "Mad Dawg!"

(STEVE *and* TOOTSIE *begin giggling and point at each other, and* STEVE *goes over to* VELMA *and sits beside her on the couch.*)

MAMMA (*Mumbles*)

Somebody always talkin' 'bout killin' somebody . . . you children shouldn't be thinkin' bout killin' some man.

POPS

What you say, Mamma?

MARCO

Well, I brought this faggot home who was workin' with us . . . one mornin' early before Franklin had gotten off. Well, I fixed breakfast for me and the cat and he had some weed so we got loaded . . .

WANDA

Marco . . . you not gonna tell me . . . ?

MARCO

Everything was nice, baby.

MARIE

Shut up, woman!

STEVE (*To* VELMA)

How're you enjoying the party?

VELMA

It's a chance to get a free drunk, ain't it?

STEVE

I guess it is as long as Marie keeps buyin' booze.

MARCO

So I got tired, see? I wanted to go to bed but this cat was there and I know I wasn't goin' ta sleep with him around me . . . so I told him to stretch out on the couch . . . ha ha ha . . . ya see Tootsie Franklin slept out there on the couch . . . so I went in my room and locked the door and went to sleep . . . heee heee heee . . .

> (MAMMA *raises her glass and begins singing and stomping the floor. Her baggy dress sweeps the floor, her slippers flap, and she reels, almost falling, between the two rooms.*)

MAMMA (*Sings*)

Said the signifyin' monkey to the lion one day . . .

POPS

There's a bad whatchamacallum comin' your way . . .

MAMMA

Mathafukker! The word's mathafukker . . . mathafukker!

> (*She spills some of her drink as she collides with* POPS.)

Yeah, let's party! It's party time . . . yeah . . . let's do the hucklebuck!

> (*She raises her skirts and does a lewd gyration.* POPS

presses against her back, holding her about her waist.)

MARIE (*To* MAMMA)

Yeah, party, baby. Yeah, go on an' party . . . you ole snag-gle-toothed, frail drunken bitch!

MARCO (*To* WANDA)

Heee heee heee . . . and Franklin finally came home and found the fag in his bed . . . heee ha ha . . .

WANDA (*To* MARIE)

She can't help herself, Aunt Marie . . . she can't help her-self.

(TOOTSIE FRANKLIN *pours fresh drinks for* SUKIE *and himself.*)

SUKIE (*To* TOOTSIE)

Marco's so funny.

TOOTSIE

Yeah, mah ole partner's always rappin' on me or Stevie Ben-son or somebody.

SUKIE

You sure are some nice guys . . . I'm glad you all moved around here.

TOOTSIE

Well, it's them . . . I don't live here . . . just be here so much I might as well, I guess . . . ha ha . . .

STEVE

Try and relax, Velma.

VELMA

Sheet!

MARCO

Now, Franklin knows this cat who's sacked out in his bed is queer . . . heee heee . . . goddamn . . . the changes Franklin went through that mornin' . . . he didn't know who to kill . . . me or the fag . . . heee heee . . . but I had my door locked and I wasn't comin' out for shit!

(*The old couple are dancing drunkenly between the rooms.*)

MAMMA

Go on and kill . . . kill . . . that's what ya should do . . . kill all tha mathafukkers!

STEVE

I'd really like to be your friend, Velma.

VELMA

Yeah, you and every other mathafukker who can get somethin' fo' nothin'.

STEVE

Awww . . . now listen, Velma. What can I do . . . huhhh? I've done all that I can do, haven't I? What can I do anymore?

VELMA

You can fill up mah glass again, Steve . . . that's what you can do.

(*Lights down*)

SCENE 4

The party.

MAMMA *sprawls upon the couch;* POPS *sleeps upon the floor beneath her feet which dangle above his head.* MONTGOMERY *dances with* VELMA. SISTER SUKIE *sits upon* MARCO's *knee, and* WANDA *and* STEVE *dance as* TOOTSIE *sits with his legs crossed at the table with* MARIE *and* MARCO.

Evening has come.

TOOTSIE (*To* MONTGOMERY)
Montgomery, don't let that young lady lose you, now.

MONTGOMERY
Son, I must confess that you young'uns are too much fo' me.

79

MARIE (*Snapping her fingers*)

Well, they may be too much for you, ole man, but I ain't seen nothin' here yet that can keep up with me.

MONTGOMERY (*Bucking his eyes and stretching mouth*)

I believe you know what ya talkin' 'bout, sister.

MARIE

Don't come sisterin' me, *brother!*

TOOTSIE

Lighten up on the ole timer, Marie Horton.

MARCO (*To* SUKIE)

All that money we made at the post office we just blew, baby . . . all that good goddamn money from all them fukkin' hours just gone . . .

MARIE (*To* WANDA)

Dance, broad, dance . . . that's a strong, good-lookin' man you out there with.

STEVE

You better believe *that!*

WANDA

Just dance, Stevie . . . that's all . . . just dance!

VELMA

Why don't you cut a step or two, Miss Marie?

MARIE (*Feeling her drinks*)

I don't see nothin' out there that looks like somethin' to me . . . what you got out there looks like death on a stick!

(TOOTSIE *laughs and slaps the table.*)

MARCO

Tootsie wouldn't see or smell Lola for two weeks . . . then come payday and there she'd be.

TOOTSIE

You gonna let Marie Horton talk to you like that, Montgomery? Oooeeee . . . heee heee. . . . The way she's down on you . . . you must be Public Fuckup Number One.

MARCO

Tootsie would give Lola *all* his money . . . *all* of it . . . I'd have to pay his carfare to work and go see Lola about givin' me enough for his rent and food money.

SUKIE

You must be lyin', Marc.

MARCO

Nawh . . . nigger come back and tell me he's in love with Lola. . . . I wonder why he have ta tell me all that . . . if he wasn't in love than he must have the worst sickness known to humanity. . . . Sheet. Many's the day I've wished I was a bitch and Tootsie Franklin was in love with me. . . . Sheet, baby, talk about somebody bein' in good shape . . . yeah, that'd be me!

STEVE (*To* MARCO)

We all get it bad sometimes.

VELMA

We all do, huh?

MARCO

Is that what you call *bad*, man?

WANDA

What would you call it, Marc?

MARCO

The Plague!

MAMMA

Cousin Marc . . . Cousin Marc . . . you sick, son?

MARCO (*Annoyed*)

Why don't you stop that shit about you bein' mah cousin, woman! You know better than that.

TOOTSIE

She's just talkin' out of her head, Marc. Leave the ole drunk alone.

SUKIE

Is Mamma yo' cousin, Marc?

MARCO

Hell, no!

STEVE

Yes, she is . . . you know Mamma doesn't lie.

MARCO

Fuck you, Stevie Benson. You big waterheaded chump.

TOOTSIE

Yeah, Marc, admit it. You know that ole drunken bag is your cousin. That's why you want to hide it so bad.

MARCO (*Peeved*)

Pawh, tell these two mathafukkers that ole drunken Mamma ain't our cousin.

(MONTGOMERY *has kissed* VELMA *when* STEVE *wasn't looking.*)

MONTGOMERY

Son, I'm not goin' to swear that you're my son, if I can help it.

(TOOTSIE *and* STEVE *laugh, as* MARCO *curses.*

VELMA *takes a seat at the table between* TOOTSIE *and* MARCO.)

MARIE (*To* VELMA)

You can do that little hootchy-kootchy dance pretty nice.

VELMA

I manage.

MAMMA

Cousin Marco . . . Cousin, come and git me . . . Cousin Marco.

MARCO

First time Tootsie and I met Stevie, Lola had just been in to stay her payday night and clean my boy Tootsie out . . .

(WANDA *sits down;* STEVE *walks into his room and begins looking over the titles of his books.*)

MARCO

Yeah . . . started when our landlady back then, Mrs. Reed, started talkin' 'bout her "nice" roomer in back.

VELMA

Well, Steve *is* a good tenant. I can vouch for that. All your landladies know you well, don't they, Stevie?

TOOTSIE

Not this one, Velma, this landlady was named Mrs. Reed . . . and boy, was Mrs. Reed somethin'. . . . Her gut stuck out so far from all that beer she and her husband, Moe, drank, you didn't know whether she was comin' or goin'.

MARCO

"That Mr. *Banton*"—wouldn't say Benson for shit—"in back has been in a terrible accident. It's just a shame." That's what she said. We didn't know that ole Stevie had gotten drunk and tore up his car.

MARIE (*To* STEVE)

You got drunk, honey?

> (O.D. *enters the rear door below, and stares groggily about. His actions indicate that he is extremely drunk.*)

MAMMA (*Delirious*)

I can't help mahself. Help me somebody.

POPS (*Mumbling*)

Yas'sum! Yas'sum!

MAMMA

Cousin . . . Lawd God Jesus . . . thank you, Father.

POPS

Yas'sum.

WANDA

Somebody should help both of them.

MARCO

I'll help them if they piss on my couch or floor. I'll put mah foot up their asses.

MONTGOMERY

Son . . . for somebody who had such a pretty and nice-tempered mamma you sometimes surprise me.

MARCO

Well, you help them, pawh. Just like you always have helped me.

WANDA

Awww . . . don't talk like that, Marco.

MARIE

Hawh . . . shit . . . that ain't right. Son talkin' to his father like that.

MARCO

Fuck him!

TOOTSIE

Hey, lighten up, Marc.

STEVE

Yeah, baby, let me light up this so we can take the weight off our . . .

(STEVE *pulls out a brown cigarette and lights it.*)

MARIE

What's that?

STEVE

Fruits of the gods, lady. Fruits of the gods.

MONTGOMERY

You know I didn't ever see mah son here, Marc, until he was in his twenties. . . . His mamma left me in Oklahoma City and came out here. Here's where I found him after she left here and went back there to stay.

MARCO

She probably heard you were comin', pawh.

(STEVE *hands* MARCO *the cigarette.*)

MONTGOMERY

It was hard knowin' each other at first, but we're more like brothers now than father and son.

MARIE

No shit.

(O.D. *begins to clamber up the front stairs after weaving through the downstairs apartment.*)

MARCO

Yeah, we met Stevie and we ain't been the same yet. This silly fucker here is enough to screw up Jesus. Everything he touches turns to shit.

STEVE

Thanks, partner.

VELMA

Is that right?

MARCO (*Passing cigarette to* MONTGOMERY)

Yeah, the only reason your ole man ain't kicked his ass is because Steve's so clumsy. One of those times Stevie took you to the Lavender Lynx, O.D. saw him come out and stand out front . . . guess you were in the can.

VELMA

You think so, Marc?

MARIE

You go to *that* place, Steve?

STEVE

Yeah, when it suits me.

SUKIE

You don't mean that . . .

TOOTSIE

Yeah, that fag joint on Washington. Stevie Benson takes Velma there because he knows that O.D. is scared silly of fags and won't be seen on the same side of the street with one.

VELMA

What he's really scared of is somebody thinkin' he's one himself . . . that's why he's out to kill me ta prove he's a man!

WANDA

Awww, Velma.

MARIE

Honey . . . don't say that.

VELMA

Why shouldn't I? He's so scared that he won't even hit Steve back because he thinks he's one.

MARCO

That's what you call strange.

MONTGOMERY

No lie.

TOOTSIE

Sheet . . . I'd kill a mathafukker come up hittin' on me.

VELMA

Yeah, most men would beat up a queer for the slightest reason, but not O.D. I don't know how that man's mind works. . . . He must think it'll rub off on him, or somethin', like chicken-pox.

MARCO

Our boy Stevie is the luckiest ass in town.

(O.D. *reaches top of the landing and falls against* STEVE's *door and sprawls upon the floor.*)

MAMMA

HAULELOUJAH! JESUS BLESS HIS NAME.

POPS

Yas'sum.

MARIE (*Drunk*)

Gawd damn . . . who's this now?

VELMA

Just O.D. . . . drunk as usual.

(*Lights down*)

SCENE 5

Night. The duplex.

Soft light shows the bedrooms of MARCO, STEVE *and* VELMA.

MARCO *reads the sports pages in bed;* WANDA *is beside him. In* STEVE's *room the back of the couch has been pushed back and made into a bed, and* MARIE HORTON *snores noisily beneath the covers.* STEVE *sits in his chair, looking moodily out front. Downstairs,* VELMA *paces about her bed, as* O.D. *stretches length-wise across it.*

WANDA

Marc, what will happen tomorrow when Aunt Marie wakes up and finds me in here with you?

MARCO

Damn . . . I don't think the Dodgers can pull it out this late in the season.

WANDA

Maybe I should go home.

(O.D. *stirs and* VELMA *stops, folds her arms and looks at him.*)

MARCO

If they can stop Mays then . . .

WANDA

I'm goin' to go home.

MARCO (*Looks at* WANDA *long*)

Don't fuck up my day completely, hear?

WANDA

But, Marc, Aunt Marie will know.

MARCO

And what do you know about Aunt Marie?

WANDA

But that's different with her.

MARCO

Yeah, it is . . . she's married.

WANDA

Maybe she'll want us to, huh? Maybe she'll want us to get married after tonight.

MARCO

Maybe she will, baby. Maybe she'll ask Stevie Benson to be the best man, and her husband, your Uncle Bob, can give you away . . . and Velma, Sukie and Mamma can be the bride's maids.

O.D. (*Raising his head and staring*)

Velma!

WANDA

She'll never let me forget this, Marco.

MARCO

Neither will she ever forget how she damn near broke her ass when we all tried to carry O.D., Mamma and Pops out of here . . . or how she cursed and ran Montgomery off and tried to fight Sukie for leavin' with Tootsie. . . . Turn off that goddamn light, Wanda. Right now I hate people.

O.D.

What you lookin' at, bitch?

WANDA

Do you have anything, Marc? I could get pregnant, you know.

VELMA

I'm lookin' at you, O.D.

MARCO

Turn off that goddamn light, like I said.

(WANDA *snaps off the light.*)

O.D.

Come here.

VELMA

I'm here all ready, O.D. All you got to do is reach out and take me.

O.D.

I said come here!

VELMA

Let me talk to you, O.D.

(O.D. *reaches over and pulls her to the bed.*)

VELMA

O.D., why?

O.D.

Open yo' legs, bitch!

VELMA

No, O.D. Steve! Steve!

(O.D. *slaps her viciously and begins strangling her. Upstairs,* STEVE *leans forward and covers his face with his hands.*)

O.D.

You're my wife, hear? You're my wife. Open your legs fo' me like you do all the rest.

VELMA (*Muffled*)
Yes, O.D.

(MARIE's *snores halt and she rolls over.*)

MARIE
Hi, baby, you got a headache, or somethin'?

(O.D. *kicks the light from the nightstand; it is black in their room, and* VELMA's *choking sobs are heard.*)

O.D. (*To the sound of love-making*)
You're my wife, ya hear. You're mine.

VELMA (*Sobbing*)
Yes, O.D. Yes, yes yes yes yes . . . O.D. . . .

(STEVE *stands and turns; he approaches* MARIE.)

MARIE
Why you lookin' like that, honey? Why?

(STEVE *sits upon the side of the couch and takes off his shoes, then snaps the light off.*)

MARIE
Baby, you shouldn't do this . . . I'm a married woman. . . .
Oh, honey, I *knew* from the first time I saw you that you
were the one. . . . Ahhh . . . honey . . . I'm right for you,
ain't I? Young man . . . you are a real young man, young
man . . . baby, if you keep on doin' that you goin' a send
me straight out that window . . .

(Silence, except for the sound of love-making which comes from the various rooms, interrupted occasionally by muffled sobs and soft whimpers.)

CURTAIN

Third Movement

SAVE ME, SAVE ME, SAVE ME, BABY

Save me, Save me, Save me, baby
Save me, Save me, Save me, baby
Save me, Save me, Save me, baby

    you say I'm mad
    but you better be
    glad
    'cause you say you
    feel fo' real
    'bout my sufferin'

Save me, Save me, Save me, baby
Save me, Save me, Save me, baby
Save me, Save me, Save me, baby

you fear I'm ah cheat
even though you
know I'm neat
so you better
get it together
fo' ya forgotten

Save me, Save me, Save me, baby
Save me, Save me, Save me, baby
Save me, Save me, Save me, baby

you suck me in
& ya string me
out
but ya know I'm
ah fool
that's not foolin'

Save me, Save me, Save me, baby
Save me, Save me, Save me, baby
Save me, Save me, Save me, baby

you jivin' round
like a shaky clown
but if that's how
you sound
I can dig it
long as it
ain't no
heavy habit

Save me, Save me, Save me, baby
Save me, Save me, Save me, baby
Save me, Save me, Save me, baby

you wanted a
woman
well I'm gonna
be the best
one I can
for bein'
anything
short of that
fo' mah money
ain't where
it's at
honey

So
Save me, Save me, Save me, baby

yes indeed
Save me, Save me, Save me, baby

& again
Save me, Save me, Save me, baby

I'm mo' woman
than you can
stand   so
take care of
business   &
don't be no
ham

Save me, etc., etc., etc.

SCENE 1

The Duplex.

VELMA *closes her door and slowly climbs the stairs and enters* STEVE's *room. He is asleep. She looks down at him for a moment, then sits upon the side of the bed, her weight awakening him.*

STEVE (*Very sleepy*)

Hey . . . how ya doin'?

VELMA

Okay.

(*Silence.*

STEVE *moves around, leans his back against the headboard.*)

101

STEVE (*Rubs eyes, yawns, scratches*)
Is it late?

VELMA
Past noon.

STEVE
No kiddin'.

VELMA
Yeah.

(*He looks at her, not smiling. Pause*)

STEVE
How many days has it been?

VELMA
Since you las' seen me?

STEVE
Yeah.

(*Silence*)

When was it?

VELMA
Three . . . four . . . days . . .

(*Pause*)

STEVE
My vacation's almost gone.

VELMA

Yeah . . . you spent most of it in bed.

STEVE

Well . . . not that much really.

VELMA

Most of it.

STEVE

How do you know . . . I haven't seen you.

VELMA

But I still knew where you were, Steve.

STEVE (*Yawns*)

Do you now?

VELMA

Since I called for you an' you didn't come you've hardly left this room, Steve.

(*Silence*)

STEVE (*Soft*)

How you been, Velma?

VELMA

Ohhh . . . I'll make it.

STEVE

Good.

VELMA

Yeah.

STEVE

I've been reading a lot.

VELMA

Yeah?

STEVE

Yeah . . . almost a book a day.

VELMA

You got a lot of brains, Stevie.

STEVE

Not really.

VELMA

Marc too.

STEVE

Yeah, Marc's the guy you better watch.

VELMA

But I got you to watch, Steve.

STEVE

Well, don't waste too much of your time on me.

(*Pause*)

VELMA

Stevie?

STEVE

Yeah.

VELMA

What do you want to be?

STEVE

Be? Hmmm . . . that's funny. . . . Well, I'll tell you. If I had my choice I'd be a reader.

VELMA

A reader?

STEVE

Yeah . . . a reader.

VELMA

You would?

STEVE

Yeah . . . I'd do nothin' all day 'cept read books I've always promised myself to read.

VELMA

What if you ran out of books? What if you had time and read all the books you ever wanted to and there were none left?

STEVE

I don't think that's possible.

VELMA

You must want to read everything in every library in the world.

STEVE

No, not quite . . . but a lot. I've always secretly planned

how if I went to jail for a long time and if they had a good library like some of the bigger places like San Quentin has . . . that I'd have lots of time to read.

VELMA

I'd never think about anything like that, Steve.

STEVE

If you wanted to read enough you would.

VELMA

I hardly ever read . . . hardly ever look at T.V. since you and Marc moved in.

STEVE

If we can take the credit for that then our visit hasn't been all bad, has it?

(*Pause*)

VELMA

It's the only thing that's kept me alive, Stevie.

(*Pause*)

STEVE

I'll never get between you and your husband again, Velma.

VELMA (*Searching*)

The only thing . . . the only thing, Steve . . .

STEVE

Never again.

(*Pause*)

VELMA

Yes, I know.

STEVE

O.D. wouldn't have ever did a tenth of what I've done to him.

VELMA

Steve?

STEVE

I know he wouldn't have.

VELMA

Steve . . . do something for me.

STEVE

What is it, Velma?

VELMA

Read somethin' to me.

STEVE

Read to you?

VELMA

Yeah.

STEVE

Okay. . . . You see that little magazine over there on my table with the red cover?

VELMA

Yeah.

STEVE

Go get it.

(*She walks to the table, picks up the magazine and brings it to* STEVE.

STEVE *takes magazine.*)

I haven't read to you in a long while.

VELMA (*Sits beside him, closer*)

No, you haven't.

STEVE (*Leafs through pages*)

This is called "In the Wine Time."

VELMA

What is it?

STEVE (*Finds place*)

"In the Wine Time."

(*He clears throat.*)

VELMA

That sounds funny . . . Reminds me of Mamma and Pops nex' door.

(*She leans forward to see the page, then lies next to him, atop the covers, her head upon his pillow, as he begins.*)

STEVE (*Reading*)

She passed the corner in small ballerina slippers, every evening during my last wine time, wearing a light summer dress with big pockets, swinging her head back and to the side all special-like, hearing a private melody singing in her head. I waited for her each dusk, and for this she granted me a smile, but on some days her selfish tune would drift out to me in a hum; we shared the smile and sad tune and met for a moment each day but one of that long summer. . . .

> (VELMA *looks at him and rests her head upon his chest.*
>
> *Lights lower and change. Music rises and the words "Save me, Save me, baby" are sung. Short interlude for the shift in time, then lights up on* VELMA *sleeping beside* STEVE *as he reads.*)

I stood listening to the barbershop taunts follow her into the darkness, watching her until the wicked city night captured her; then I turned back to meet autumn and Cliff and Lou in our last wine time, meeting the years which had to hurry hurry so I could begin the search that I have not completed.

> (STEVE *crawls from under the covers on the other side of the bed. He has on shorts and puts on his pants as* VELMA *wakes.*)

VELMA

You finished already?

STEVE

Yeah.

VELMA

I liked it.

STEVE

Thanks.

VELMA

You read so good.

STEVE (*Puts shirt on*)

No, not really.

(*Pause*)

VELMA (*Still on bed*)

Steve . . . I'm going to have a baby.

(*Pause*)

STEVE

You are?

VELMA

I'm three months gone, Steve.

STEVE

Are you sure?

VELMA

I'm sho.

STEVE

That's too bad.

VELMA

Until the other night O.D. hasn't touched me in months.

STEVE

You're sure of that?

VELMA

I wouldn't let him . . . not after he came from his woman.

STEVE

Look . . . Velma . . . let's talk about it later.

VELMA

Okay, Stevie. I got to go anyway.

STEVE

I'll see you later, huh?

VELMA

Okay.

(*She goes to the door, looks before she steps out, then exits.*

Lights lower.)

SCENE 2

The duplex.

That evening.

Light on in MARCO'S *room. He,* TOOTSIE *and* STEVE *complete a game of cards.*

          TOOTSIE (*Turns cards face-up*)
Well, Marc . . . you did it that time.

          MARCO
Yeah . . . it's about time.

          TOOTSIE
Too bad, Stevie.

STEVE (*Tosses down cards*)

Yeah . . . too bad.

MARCO (*To* STEVE)

What's up, shithead?

STEVE

Up?

(STEVE *gets up and walks to the window and looks
out.*)

MARCO

Yeah . . . up.

TOOTSIE

See her comin' yet? Heee heee . . .

STEVE (*Turns back*)

That's none of your business.

MARCO

Oh . . . sorry.

STEVE (*Perceiving*)

Hey, man . . . I didn't mean that.

TOOTSIE

She left this mornin' to go shoppin', she said. Passed me as
I came in. Sho was a boss dress she had on. . . . Probably
was goin' down and see O.D. on his job . . . the way she
was dressed.

———

MARCO

You should know, Franklin . . . much as your ole lady, Lola, used to come see . . .

STEVE

Look . . . I don't want nobody talkin' about that.

TOOTSIE (*Grins*)

About Lola?

MARCO

You don't?

(STEVE *turns back to the window.* MARCO *and* TOOTSIE *look at one another;* TOOTSIE *cracks up and begins giggling.*)

MARCO

Hey . . . Franklin, Steve don't want you to be talkin' about that.

TOOTSIE (*Giggles*)

Heee heee . . . hey, man . . . hey, Marc . . . stop it . . .

MARCO

Stop it? I ain't gigglin' like a jackass . . . am I, Hanky-Panky? Am I?

TOOTSIE

Heee heee . . . oh, man . . . heee heee . . . I ain't talkin' 'bout dat . . . you know it.

MARCO

Then what are you talkin' about, man?

(TOOTSIE *doubles over from laughter*.)

STEVE
Hey, man, why don't you guys forget it.

MARCO
Yeah, man . . . we'll forget it. . . . Won't we, Franklin?

TOOTSIE (*Laughs*)
Ohhh . . . ohhhh god . . . I'm gonna bust my sides. . . .
You gonna kill me, Stevie Benson.

MARCO
Steve . . . you gonna kill Franklin?

TOOTSIE
Ahhh . . . Marc . . . why don't you quit it? I can't take
anymore.

STEVE (*Sits down*)
C'mon . . . let's play another game.

(*Both* MARCO *and* TOOTSIE *laugh*.)

TOOTSIE
Steve . . . Steve . . . heee heee . . . tell us . . . hee hee
. . . please tell us how you got yourself in dis mess, man?

MARCO (*Laughs*)
Man . . . Tootsie, man . . . you tryin' to say that our
boy Stevie . . . hee hee . . . is a fuck-up?

TOOTSIE
Oh, man . . . dis po' nigger's gonna get his self killed.

STEVE

Ah, man, c'mon an' deal.

(O.D. *and* VELMA *enter downstairs, carrying grocery packages.*)

VELMA

That's not too heavy for you, is it, honey?

O.D.

Nawh.

VELMA

Here, put them down here, baby. . . . Are ya hungry?

STEVE

There's things you two don't understand . . . that's all.

MARCO

What don't we understand, shithead?

TOOTSIE

I know what I don't understand.

MARCO

Quiet, Franklin . . . Steve said you didn't understand.

VELMA

O.D., I could fix your dish tonight . . . ham hocks and limas. . . . How bout it, honey?

O.D.

Nawh . . . I don't want any damn beans.

TOOTSIE

I don't understand what this is all about. I never understood it from the first, man.

VELMA

What do you want, O.D.? Huh, honey?

O.D.

Nothin' . . . I'm goin' out tonight.

STEVE

Look . . . let me tell you somethin'.

TOOTSIE

We listenin'.

STEVE

You know I'm in this thing with the girl downstairs, right?

MARCO

Yeah . . . the landlady.

STEVE

That's right.

TOOTSIE

Yeah . . . you messin' round with Velma.

STEVE

Yeah . . . we all know that.

MARCO

Yeah, we know.

STEVE

Then why you want to give me such a hard time?

TOOTSIE

Hard time? Look man . . .

STEVE

I love her.

MARCO

You love her?

TOOTSIE

Who?

STEVE

I love her . . . and I'm going to get her.

TOOTSIE

Now look, man . . . I don't want to be gettin' into your business but you actin' plumb dumb.

MARCO

Yeah, like a fool, man.

STEVE

I might be a fool to you . . . but I know what I'm doin'. I'm doin' what I have to do.

MARCO

Look . . . Stevie Benson . . .

STEVE

I'm doin' what I have to do. What I must do.

MARCO

Listen to me, man . . . leave that woman alone, you hear me. Leave that little black bitch alone.

STEVE

Hey, Marco . . . don't be talkin' like that.

MARCO

How you want me to talk? What am I'm supposed to say when I see you gettin' ready to fuck up, huh?

TOOTSIE

Now if that's what he wants to do, Marc . . .

MARCO

Now you supposed to be gettin' yourself together, Steve. . . . You bustin' your balls to get through school . . . you ain't no dope even though you act like a fool most of the time . . .

STEVE

That's none of your business.

MARCO

It is when it jeopardizes me . . . I live here too, remember? And I don't want that woman's big ape-lookin' husband to get any wrong ideas. Now listen to me, man . . . look . . . I'm ten times better lookin' than you, right?

TOOTSIE (*Giggles*)

Stevie . . . I wouldn't play that.

MARCO

Admit it! I'm ten times as handsome as Stevie Benson here. Right? Well, we all can't be good lookin' . . .

STEVE

What you tryin' to say, Marc?

MARCO

I'm tryin' to say that when the deal goes down, O.D. might decide to put his foot up my ass on G.P. . . . 'cause he don't like me . . .

TOOTSIE

'Cause he might not like pretty-boy curly-headed niggers around his ole lady.

MARCO

Exactly! And when he finds out you fuckin' his ole lady . . . he just might get it into his monkey brain to come upstairs and take care of this pretty yaller nigger that lives with you, Stevie Benson. You know . . . he might think I'm gettin' some of his stuff too.

STEVE

Awwww . . . now look, man . . .

MARCO

Now I know you, Steve.

STEVE

You don't know me. . . . Nobody knows me . . . what's in my mind and guts . . . how my breath stops in my throat and chokes me when I hear my woman call out at night . . . call out to me.

She's not your woman, idiot!

Nobody knows the love and beauty I find in holding my woman in my arms. . . . My woman . . . a poor little scared black girl that's even dumber than I'm supposed to be. Nobody knows that I don't care if she has kids . . . children who will hate me forever if I get her like I plan. Nor will anybody know that she'll never know me . . . really know me . . . this black man . . . with this mind . . . they'll never understand the thoughts that flash through my head and scorch the back of my eyes . . . these eyes that see her being beaten and raped, these eyes that see the flames of the hell that we all live in . . . live our black lives in here . . . in our cool dark little lives . . . getting ready to become something we ain't now or will never be . . . really. Some names like what? Colored insurance man, postal clerk, negro journalist, teacher, lawyer, afro-american dentist, actor, horn blower, whiskey pourer . . . clown? Don't marry anything black . . . at least not as dark and down and womanly as she . . . don't think of it, with her you say, nigger . . . why . . . why? Because she's nobody . . . a little black female nothing with babies that she don't even know how they came so fast . . . and she shouldn't be in my together program anyway 'cause I'm due for greater things. Yeah . . . greater things . . . ha ha. . . . Well I'm not, you know . . . not due, that is . . . not due for anything more than what I'm due for now . . . and that is only to be a nigger . . . or be black . . . nothing short of those two absolutes. To work in this whiteman's land . . . or build one of my own . . . to give a last ditch try to save my balls. . . . And to make some children so that they can climb up over my bloated sweating carcass once it falls . . . falls in the service of them . . . That we call progress . . . ha ha ha . . . don't get too close to her because she's not going anywhere . . . or at least in the same direction that we are, right, Marc? But where in the hell are we going, brother? Where? Into the machine maze of I.B.M. . . . Into the confines of teaching the slavemaster's offspring . . . into the insanity of thinking we can teach them their own language . . . my poor brother, language is more than words . . . it is deeds and gestures . . . and silence . . . what history can we teach those who hide from history . . . those who believe their lies and fears create history . . . can we teach them their own sterility of soul that we slaves learned better than they that call it their civilization . . .

MARCO

Stop ranting! Stop raving, will you? Have you lost your mind?

TOOTSIE

Hey, man . . . I didn't know you were a preacher.

STEVE

Yeah . . . I preach . . . I preach when I get ready. I preach that we are people. We are niggers . . . we are black. . . . We are whatever we are . . . and my woman has black skin and thick lips and a wide nose and healthy flat feet that she got from her cotton-pickin' mamma and daddy. . . . And she's got troubles with her tubes from havin' too many children too soon. . . . But she's mine and I'm not abandoning her . . . I'm not leaving her with a crippled beast that would kill her because she merely loves him . . . and hates her for offering herself to him . . . the father of her babies.

TOOTSIE (*Giggles*)

Man . . . this is really gettin' deep . . . this is too heavy fo' me.

(*Lights down*)

SCENE 3

Lights show VELMA *and* O.D. *in their apartment.*

VELMA *blocks the door.*

O.D.

Get away from that door . . . bitch . . .

VELMA

No, O.D. . . . . I'm not.

O.D.

You crazy or somethin', woman?

VELMA

Stay home with me tonight, O.D. . . . . Please stay with me tonight.

O.D.

Get out of the way.

No, O.D. . . . Stop!

(They struggle. VELMA *keeps her place, blocking the door.)*

Just one night. One night with me, O.D. With me. Don't go to her one night, please, baby. . . . That's all I ask. Please, O.D.

O.D.

I'm not gonna tell you anymore to get out of the way, Velma.

VELMA

If I don't get out of the way what are you gonna do to me? What, O.D.? You've already done your worse by me. . . . Everything now is just different keys on the same piano . . .

(He slaps her.)

Go head . . . do it again . . . do it again, if it makes you feel good, O.D.!

O.D.

What'cha gonna do . . . call your boyfriend upstairs? What'cha gonna do . . . scream for Stevie?

VELMA

I don't need nobody to handle you, O.D. You ain't even man enough for that, O.D. . . . you a punk, man . . . a faggot!

(Screams)

(O.D. *takes a knife from his pocket and slashes her arm that she holds the doorknob with.*

She clutches at her bleeding arm and falls and crouches to the floor.

VELMA *cries, frightened and hysterical.*)

O.D. . . . O.D., you're crazy! O.D. . . . Oh, please God . . . help me!

(*He pushes her away from the door with his foot, opens it and leaves.*

VELMA *screams.*)

O.D.! . . . O.D.! . . . Please . . . please, baby, please . . . O.D.! Oh God, let my poor black ass die now . . . oh Lord . . . oh, Lord God have mercy!

(*Sounds offstage.* MAMMA'*s,* POPS' *and* SUKIE'*s voices. Running feet.*

As VELMA *faints,* STEVE *enters. Seeing the wound, he tries to stop it while cradling her.*)

STEVE

It's alright now, baby. . . . It's okay now . . . everything's okay, Velma. . . . Baby . . . I love you . . . I love you . . . and I ain't gonna let nothin' more happen to you.

MAMMA (*Enters*)

Oh Lawd . . . I knew it! (*Screams*) I knew it! Oh Lawd in God's Heaven have mercy!

(SUKIE *and* POPS *enter*)

SUKIE

Mamma . . . Mamma, has somethin' terrible happened?

MAMMA (*Cries*)

She's dead . . . my po' baby's dead. Velma's dead!

POPS

Oh my . . . oh my my my my . . . how terrible.

STEVE

Somebody help me . . . will you give me a hand with her?

(*Lights down*)

SCENE 4

Later that night.

VELMA, MAMMA *and* SUKIE *sit in* VELMA's *apartment.*

SUKIE *and* VELMA *sip beer.* MAMMA *has wine. The radio plays.*

MAMMA
But what you gonna do, girl?

VELMA
Nothin'. What can I do?

SUKIE
You can get out of here, Velma.

VELMA

Get out? Nawh, I couldn't do that.

MAMMA

But why, Velma? Why?

SUKIE

The way he's messin' around he's out to kill you, girl . . .
you know that, don't cha?

VELMA

Nawh . . . he wouldn't do that. O.D. ain't got no sense but
he wouldn't do nothin' like that.

MAMMA

I just can't understand you. Shoot . . . I know I wouldn't
let no nigger be half killin' and cuttin' on me.

SUKIE

Me neither. If there was any bleedin' to be done . . . it
wouldn't be me, Mamma. Shit, I'd keep a pot of grease boilin'
on the stove for somebody like that.

VELMA

You know . . . this is the only real home I've had.

MAMMA

When I met Pops he thought he'd stand up on his rare legs
. . . yes, indeed he did . . .

VELMA

First time I've ever sunk roots this deep.

SUKIE

I had an ole nigger man once. Thought he was bad.

MAMMA

Called himself "Dawg" then . . . leastwise that's what his
no-count friends used to called him . . . not so long ago
neither.

VELMA

Even when I was back home . . . that wasn't like home . . .
really. That was just my mamma and daddy's place. I just
lived there.

SUKIE

I told that man, "Nigger! If you ever look at me funny
you gonna be sorry . . . you gonna be sorry for the day
you was born." Yeah . . . that's what I told that nigger.

MAMMA

Clifton Slaughter Dawson . . . that's his name . . . his real
name. But I just call him Pops now . . . like everybody
else . . . not even "Dawg." Ha ha ha . . . "Ole Dawg"
. . . that's what I'd call him . . . was my special name for
him.

VELMA

Lived there when O.D. was in the service. Nobody wanted us
to get married . . . 'specially mamma. But when she found
out I was pregnant the first time . . . that woman threat-
ened to call O.D.'s commanding officer, if he didn't do something about "the situation."

SUKIE

But he sure knew how to treat me . . . made me feel real

good all the time we was together. Real good, chile. Never did know why the mathafukker left . . . good as I was to him.

MAMMA

"Ole Dawg" was some hunk of a man in his day. . . . That was before I met him, of course. I only saw the tail-end of the real "Dawg." He won't tell me much about it . . . but that man was somethin' . . . hmmmp . . . you wouldn't know it to look at him . . . would you?

VELMA

But we got married . . . and I stayed with mamma . . . and O.D. gave me a baby everytime he'd come home on leave.

MAMMA

Sometimes I wish I had met him sooner. . . . Before we were both old and fallin' apart. I know we wouldn't be on this wine if we had gotten together when we still had young ideas about something . . . instead of just clogged-up lumps for minds. If we had met when we was young . . . when we was strong and could depend on our backs to carry us where we was goin' and support each other on the way it might have been nice. But nothin' right ever happens like that . . . to us. I was where I was . . . and he was off doin' other things. Sometimes he tells me about his wife back then . . . Brenda . . . yeah, Ole Dawg was married . . . wouldn't think it, now would you? But he was . . . even had a little boy . . . boy named Clifton . . . after him. Yeah, the ole fart tells about everything he knows when he gets some of this poison in him. He even cries . . . yeah, cries on my ole dried-up breasts. Poor Ole Dawg . . . cries and tells me how he's goin' to go find his son one day. That's what he wants to do, he sez. See young Cliff a man . . . with his own eyes

before they get too old. Before Ole Dawg dies . . . dies
drunk . . . like an ole drunken puppy.

VELMA

I wanted to get away . . . start my own home. I would always tell O.D. . . . "O.D.," I'd say, "O.D., let's get an
apartment somewheres . . . let's move. Not into town or
over by your people . . . but away to a big city. . . . Like
New York . . . or Washington . . . or Chicago or San
Francisco . . . or even Hollywood." Yeah . . . that's what
I'd tell him, but all he ever said was, "Baby, it ain't time
yet." It ain't time, he'd say . . . and there I was sittin' on
that farm all mah life, havin' babies and gettin' more stuck
there. So when he came out of the service I told him if he
didn't get up and take me out of there . . . I'd be gone one
mornin'. I'd be long gone . . . just me. Let him and my
mamma and my ole daddy take care of the kids. They could
do it better than I could anyway, 'cause I all the time had
the city on my mind. But I finally got him to go. He saw it
in my eyes . . . my mamma did too. So we was supposed to
come out here for a while and see how it was. . . . O.D.
wanted to go to school. And he did. Nigger got a good job,
which surprised me. And I had a home of my own. . . . But
by then I had lost O.D.

> (STEVE *steps upon the porch from the street, out-*
> *side. He peers at* VELMA's *door, then holds on to*
> *the porch railing, obviously drunk.*)

SUKIE

I'm gonna get me a man one day. A man I know will be
mine. I ain't goin'a be goin' for this stuff of any ole piss-ass
man comin' along and takin' advantage of me. Yeah, I'm
goin' to get one. But I ain't goin' to take no stuff off him.

He's gonna have to treat me like I'm somethin'. Like I'm a lady. Or I'll cut his damn throat. . . . Yeah, that's right. I'd rather stay alone until judgment day than have a man with me who don't know who I am. I hope ahm gonna die if that man wouldn't have to sleep with one eye open all his days if he messed with me. I'll take care of him, if I have to, I'll have his kids . . . stick with him through grit and gravy . . . but I ain't takin' no stuff.

(STEVE *knocks, then pushes the door open and looks in.*)

VELMA

What chou lookin' at?

STEVE (*Drunk*)

Who? . . . Me?

VELMA (*Disgust*)

Ohhh . . . don't come with that. C'mon in here and shut the door.

(*He enters.*)

MAMMA

Hi, Stevie.

STEVE

Why hallo, Mamma. Hi, Sukie.

SUKIE

Hello, Stevie.

VELMA (*Accusing*)

You been drinkin', Stevie!

STEVE

Drinking? Me?

VELMA

Yeah . . . you're drunk.

STEVE

Wahl . . . just a little bit.

MAMMA

Ahhh, Velma. Ain't no harm in somebody drinkin'.

SUKIE

You do it all the time, don't cha, Mamma?

MAMMA

Yeah, girl . . . I'd be lost without my pick-me-up.

STEVE

Wahl . . . if you say I'm drunk . . . then I guess I'm drunk.

(*He sits down heavily at the table.*)

VELMA

Watch mah furniture, man.

STEVE (*To* VELMA)

You really lookin' pretty tonight, baby.

VELMA

Awww, man . . . why don't you shut up.

MAMMA

Now that ain't nice, Velma.

SUKIE

Don't be that way, Velma. Wish somebody would say things
to me like that.

STEVE

You would, Sukie? Well, I think you're lookin' pretty good
tonight too.

VELMA

Where you been tonight, Steve?

SUKIE

You don't mean that, do you?

STEVE

Sure I do. Not as good as you-know-who here . . . but
pretty foxy still . . .

MAMMA

There's nothin' wrong with drinkin' that I can see. Ain't
never hurt me.

SUKIE (*Stands, models*)

You like this dress, Steve? I got it on sale downtown.

(STEVE *spies something on the table. He brushes at
it.*)

VELMA

That roach didn't come from here.

STEVE

I didn't say . . .

MAMMA

I can drink anything I want and hold it better'n anybody
I know.

VELMA

I keep my place too clean to let those things in. Since you
and Marco moved in I been seein' them. You probably brought
them in with you.

STEVE

Roaches?

SUKIE

Look, yawhl . . . I got to be goin' . . .

VELMA

Why, girl? The way you and Stevie's hittin' it off I thought
you'd be spendin' the evenin'.

SUKIE (*Indignant*)

Well, I came over here to see you, Velma. You know I was
invited by you and nobody else. Somethin's wrong with this
place . . . I'm leavin'.

MAMMA

Ain't you gonna finish your beer, dear?

(SUKIE *exits.*)

STEVE

You know I've seen roaches from one end of this country to
the next.

MAMMA

Yeah? So have I.

VELMA

Well . . . I haven't!

STEVE

No?

VELMA

At least not in my house.

STEVE

Ya know . . . that's a lot of bullshit, Velma.

VELMA

You callin' me a liar, Stevie . . . with your drunk self.

(CROOK *comes up on the porch and enters the house
without knocking at door.*)

MAMMA

Oh mah lawd . . . who's that?

STEVE (*Still drunk*)

We all seen roaches . . . all of us. Most of us have had them.

VELMA

What chou doin' walkin' into my house without knocking,
Crook?

(CROOK *says nothing, but saunters around looking
about and into the rooms and observing them.*)

STEVE

I ain't never known no black people that had no experience with roaches . . . unless they was in England or somewheres.

MAMMA (*Rises*)

I think I hear Pops callin'. I got to be leavin' now.

VELMA

Bye, Mamma.

(MAMMA *exits out the back.*)

STEVE (*Noticing* CROOK)

Hey . . . who's this?

VELMA

One of my watchdogs . . . right, Crook?

(CROOK *smiles out of the side of his mouth.*)

STEVE

Watchdog?

VELMA

Well, ain't cha, Crook?

STEVE

What's he watchin'?

VELMA

Didn't your master O.D. send you around here to check . . .

STEVE (*To* CROOK)

Hey, man . . . what the fuck you think you doin'?

(*Surprise shows on* CROOK's *face; he puts his hand in his pocket.*)

VELMA

Get the hell out of here, Crook.

STEVE (*Rises, his condition mean*)

Did you hear what I just said . . . mathafukker!

(CROOK *moves against a wall and watches* STEVE.)

VELMA

You've had your look, Crook. Now go on and report like the good little stooge you are. . . . Get out of mah house.

CROOK (*Sullen*)

O.D. pays rent here.

STEVE (*Advancing*)

You gonna act bad . . . ain't chou!

VELMA (*Frightened*)

You heard what I said, Crook. . . . And Steve . . . keep out of this. This ain't none of your business.

STEVE

Well, I'm gonna make it my business.

CROOK (*To* STEVE)

Think you can?

STEVE (*Well-oiled and spoiling*)

I'm gonna enjoy puttin' mah foot in your ass, punk!

(VELMA *pulls a large carving knife from the table drawer.*)

VELMA

I said get out of here, Crook. You too, Steve. You can go through my room and up the stairs to your place. Crook! Leave the way you came.

STEVE

When he goes, I go.

VELMA

Get out of here, Crook. . . . Or they gonna take your body out of here.

(CROOK *moves toward the door, still facing them.*)

CROOK (*To* STEVE)

I ain't gonna forget you, brother. O.D. thinks somethin' wrong with you . . . but I know what's happenin'.

STEVE (*For* VELMA*'s benefit*)

Jump anytime you want, man. I'm just layin' for you.

(CROOK *leaves.*)

VELMA

And now you get some sleep.

STEVE

Hey, baby, you don't . . .

VELMA

Go home, Steve!

STEVE

Hey, why don't you come up for . . .

VELMA

I don't want to see you no more, Steve . . . ever.

STEVE

Oh.

(*He turns and exits.*)

SCENE 5

That same night in the duplex.

The house is dark except for the few sources of nightlight.

A figure cautiously enters from the street, crosses the porch and stealthily climbs the stairs to MARCO's *and* STEVE's *flat.*

Lights rise slowly to show CROOK *standing outside of* STEVE's *door. He opens it and peers in. Then he slips inside.*

Lights reveal STEVE *asleep in his bed.* CROOK *takes a knife from his pocket and opens it. He moves toward* STEVE.

Downstairs, TOOTSIE FRANKLIN *enters noisily and climbs the stairs to upstairs.*

Hearing TOOTSIE's *approach,* CROOK *hides behind the door.*

TOOTSIE *enters, after giving a couple of knocks on the door.*

TOOTSIE

Hey . . . anybody here?

(*Sees* STEVE)

Hey, man . . . you sleep?

(TOOTSIE *walks halfway into the room and* CROOK *attempts to sneak out.*

Sees CROOK's *shadow and turns.*)

Hey! . . . WHO YOU?

(TOOTSIE *grabs the back of* CROOK's *collar.* CROOK *squirms about and slashes at him but misses.*

TOOTSIE *throws him down the stairs. At the bottom* CROOK *gains his feet and flees.*)

STEVE (*Groggy*)

What's going on?

TOOTSIE

Hey, Steve . . . who was that cat in here with a knife?

STEVE (*Rising*)

Knife?

TOOTSIE

Yeah . . . the mathafukker I jest kicked down your stairs.

STEVE

Are you serious, man?

TOOTSIE *(Hands him something)*

If he was a dream then it's the first one whose collar came off when I snatched him, man . . . hee heee heee . . .

STEVE *(Looking at material)*

Damn, Tootsie, man . . . damn . . . goa-d damn!

(Lights down)

Fourth Movement

COOL BLOWIN'

When you know
right
but do
wrong
when you climb
out on
that last limb
you know
it won't
be long
befo'
cool blowin'

don't blow your cool
don't blow your cool
don't blow your cool

don't blow your cool
and be no fool

When reality
takes you
to "A"
but your
head goes
to "Z"
& your eyes
see light
but your
mind's
not yet
on "B"
that's
cool blowin'

don't blow your cool
don't blow your cool
don't blow your cool

don't blow your cool
and be no fool

When the floor
falls away
and you ain't
got no wings
and the sky
cracks . . . open
and you sing
Ah'm doin'
mah thing
well . . .
it's some more
cool blowin'
yeah cool blowin'
don't blow your cool
fool
yeah cool blowin'
oooooooooooo
oooooooooooo
oooooooooooo

blowin'.

SCENE 1

Two days later. Noon.

MARCO *sits in his bed, his back against the head-board, reading the paper.*

STEVE *and* VELMA *stand on the downstairs porch, outside* VELMA's *door.* VELMA *opens her door and steps in; she turns and* STEVE *pushes his head through the cracked door and kisses her.*

He climbs the stairs, walks through his room and knocks on MARCO's *door.*

Downstairs VELMA *stretches out on her bed and turns out the light.*

Yeah . . . who's there?

(STEVE *steps inside.*)

Hey . . . buddy buddy . . . how ya doin'? . . . Where you been keepin' yourself?

> (STEVE *says nothing but takes a small gun out of his pocket and pushes it toward* MARCO, *as if showing it to him.*
>
> *Uneasy*)

Steve . . . Hey, man, is that a gun? . . . Don't point that thing at me.

STEVE

Man . . . there ain't nothin' to worry about.

> (*The gun fires; the slug digs a hole in the wall above and behind* MARCO's *head.*
>
> *Silence.*
>
> *Downstairs,* VELMA *rises, snaps on the light; her expression is startled; she goes to the hallway.*)
>
> (*Shocked*)

Damn, man . . .

> (MARCO *slides down in the bed.* STEVE *looks at gun, stunned.*)

Wow, man . . . I didn't know it was cocked.

MARCO (*Scared*)
You didn't know it was cocked! You simple shit!

VELMA (*Downstairs*)

STEVE . . . STEVIE . . . IS ANYTHING WRONG?

STEVE (*Puts gun in pocket*)

I didn't know it would go off.

MARCO (*Shakes*)

You didn't know . . . shit!

(*He rises and begins to dress.*)

He didn't know . . . goddamn . . . why did I have to pick this simple motherfucker of all people for a roommate . . . of all the silly-lookin' fucks in the world . . . accident had to bring us together.

VELMA (*Begins climbing stairs*)

Steve!

STEVE (*Walks to doorway*)

Everything's okay, baby! We was just playin' around.

VELMA

Oh . . . is that all?

STEVE

Yeah . . . go on back down, baby. I'll see you later.

VELMA (*Descends*)

O.K. . . . I'll see you tonight, honey.

MARCO

Honey . . . baby . . . you and the landlady sound like you runnin' a honeymoon hotel.

STEVE

Yeah . . . guess we do.

MARCO

Say, roommate . . . where is this all going to end?

STEVE

End?

MARCO

Yeah . . . this famous trio of you . . . the landlady . . . and the landlady's big husband . . . "Hamfists."

STEVE

Awww . . . well . . . don't let it worry you.

MARCO

Oh . . . I should be cool and calm . . .

STEVE

That's right.

MARCO

I should be together . . . very detached and emotionally collected.

STEVE

That's right. . . . Just be cool.

MARCO

Like just now . . . when after I've nearly gotten my brains blown out.

STEVE

It was an accident, Marc.

MARCO

I'd still be dead.

STEVE

Things like that don't happen often.

MARCO

Hey . . . what the hell you doin' with a gun?

STEVE

We just got 'em.

MARCO

We just got them?

STEVE

Yeah . . . Velma and me.

MARCO

Wait a minute! What you're sayin' is that you and the land-lady have gone out and bought pistols.

STEVE

Yeah . . . never tell when you might need them.

MARCO

Who said that . . . you or Velma?

STEVE

We both thought that.

MARCO

And you got these pop guns in a store.

Yeah.

MARCO

And you registered them with the police department.

STEVE

That's the law.

(*Silence.*

MARCO *looks at him a long moment, then lights a cigarette.*

The radio plays a Ray Charles ballad.)

MARCO

Say, man . . . I don't want you to start thinkin' anything's wrong or anything . . . but I'm goin' to start lookin' for someplace else to live.

STEVE

Well . . . okay, Marc . . . if that's how you feel.

(VELMA *comes to the bottom of the staircase.*)

VELMA

Steve! Marco! Hey, Steve and Marco! I'm gettin' ready to fix dinner. Would you like to have dinner with me?

STEVE (*To* MARCO)

How 'bout it?

VELMA

Hey . . . are ya home?

MARCO (*Shrugs*)

Why not?

STEVE (*Goes to top of stairs*)

Hi, landlady.

VELMA

Hello? . . . You're comin', huh?

STEVE

You better believe it.

(*Lights down*)

SCENE 2

That evening in the duplex.

MAMMA *and* POPS *sit in* VELMA'*s apartment and drink wine.*

MARCO, STEVE *and* TOOTSIE *play cards at the downstairs table.*

VELMA *is busy about the house.*

MARCO

Damn . . . ain't I ever gonna have a good night against you two fucks?

TOOTSIE

Awww, man . . . you ain't doin' so bad. It's Stevie who's losin' . . . as usual.

MARCO

Sheet.

STEVE

You can say that again, Franklin.

MARCO

Sheeet.

VELMA (*Dusting*)

Is that what you do with all your money, Steve?

MARCO

What money?

VELMA

Now you not tellin' me that Stevie don't have no money . . . are you, Marco?

MARCO

Now you should know . . . landlady.

TOOTSIE

Heee heee . . . why don't you check yourself, man?

MAMMA

Stevie and Velma look so good together.

STEVE

Deal . . . won't cha?

POPS

Sho do . . . sho do . . . they looks good together.

(SUKIE *steps up on the porch and knocks at* VELMA's *door.*)

VELMA

Come in.

MARCO

Damn . . . whose deal is it.

STEVE

Yours.

SUKIE

I thought I'd stop in . . . since I was passin' by. Is that okay?

VELMA

C'mon in, girl.

MARCO

Can't be my deal. . . . It couldn't have gone around that fast.

TOOTSIE

Why hello, Miss Sukie Mae.

SUKIE

Hi, Tootsie.

POPS

I think Stevie and Velma look good together . . . that's right . . . good.

STEVE

Why don't you forget about Stevie and Velma . . . huh?

MAMMA

He ain't sayin' nothin' wrong, Stevie.

VELMA

What chou been doin', girl?

SUKIE

Oh . . . livin' through it. Just livin' through it. How you been?

VELMA

Same ole same.

MARCO

Go head and deal, Steve.

STEVE

Man . . . you know it's your deal.

POPS

I can't help what Stevie and Velma do . . . I ain't their husband.

STEVE (*Half-rises*)

What did you say?

TOOTSIE

Relax, Steve. Can't you see the ole man is drunk out of his head?

MARCO (*Smiling*)

What's happen'n, buddy buddy? You not losin' your cool, are you?

VELMA

Steve?

MAMMA

He ain't done nothin', Steve.

VELMA

Steve?

POPS

Nawh . . . I ain't done nothin'. . . . I don't care what you and Velma do, Stevie. . . . It's your business.

STEVE

Shut up, old man!

TOOTSIE

Hey, man . . . there ain't no need for that.

STEVE (*Threatening*)

Shut up, Tootsie!

TOOTSIE (*Rises*)

Hey, man . . . what's wrong? Remember? If it wasn't for me you wouldn't be here.

VELMA

What's he talkin' 'bout, Steve?

MARCO (*Points at* STEVE)

That reminds me . . . because of this nigger I was nearly not here too. . . . He almost shot me in the head.

STEVE

Lissen . . . all yawhl. I just came down here to play cards.

VELMA

What? You forget about all that food you ate already?

SUKIE

Sheet. . . . I knew I shoulda kept mah ass at home.

POPS (*Gets up, staggering*)

I'm goin' . . .

MAMMA

So am I . . . wait for me, ole man.

VELMA

Yeah . . . go on an' get some sleep . . . yawhl.

POPS (*Turns in doorway, wobbles*)

Steve . . . you and Velma and O.D. act too crazy for me to stay 'round yawhl.

> (POPS *staggers out to the porch.* STEVE *gets up to follow him;* VELMA *blocks his way.*
>
> MARIE *and* WANDA *walk up onto the porch.*)

VELMA

Forget it, honey. We ain't got nothin' to worry about. That's what we bought the guns for.

MARIE (*Stands at door to go upstairs*)

Why, hello, Steve. . . . We came by to see Marco. Is he in?

POPS (*Standing between the groups on the porch.*)

And Velma, your husband might come back . . . and catch me with you.

> (STEVE *shoves* VELMA *out of his way.*)

160

MAMMA (*Protecting* POPS)

Steve . . . now you leave him the fuck alone.

(STEVE *pushes past* MAMMA.)

I'm warnin' you, Steve.

POPS

Steve . . . I ain't said nothin' 'bout you and Velma. I don't care . . .

(*Steve slaps the old man, knocking him back against the house.* POPS *attempts to keep his balance but* STEVE *slaps him once more, knocking him down on the porch.*)

MARIE

Goddamn . . . what the hell's going on?

(*There is a general protest against* STEVE.)

MAMMA (*Crying*)

You dirty no-count mathafukker! You lousy little sonna bitch!

(STEVE *pushes past her and* VELMA, *and re-enters the first floor, past* MARCO *and* TOOTSIE *who look at* POPS *through the door.*)

VELMA (*Following*)

Steve! No, Steve . . . talk to me, please, honey.

MAMMA

Yo ah lousy little nigger dawg, Steve Benson!

WANDA *(On porch)*

Marc . . . Marc! Are you in there?

MARCO *(From doorway)*

Can't you see me?

WANDA

Oh . . . Tootsie was in the way.

MAMMA

I hope O.D. tears yo throat out . . . you low-down matha-fukker! yo ah dawg . . . that's all you are . . . yo know that, don't cha?

MARIE *(Impatient)*

We're going upstairs, Marc. I can't stand all this foolish-ness. Tell Steve where we're at . . . if and when he gets him-self together.

(Commands)

C'mon, Wandie.

(They start up the stairs.

STEVE *and* VELMA *stand on the first floor, silently eyeing one another.*

SUKIE *and* MAMMA *help* POPS *off the porch; he has wet his pants from the shock of his beating, and is dazed. They exit with cries, curses and soothing comforts for* POPS.

MARCO *shakes his head and mutters under his breath while* TOOTSIE *shrugs, scratches his head and giggles.*

O.D. *enters the rear first-floor door and slams it behind him.*

Seeing him, STEVE *walks calmly toward him.* O.D.*'s face is blank, but at the last moment he smiles slightly, before* STEVE *punches him squarely in the face with all his might.*

O.D. *falls back against the wall. And* STEVE *follows him like a good boxer and jabs and punches him around the head and body in well-executed flurries of punches.*

MARCO *gasps when the first punch lands and turns and flees from the house, out the porch doorway, and away in the direction of the street.*

TOOTSIE *watches with amazement upon his face.*

With a smile on her face, VELMA *sits down in a chair on the other side of the room and looks on.*

Upstairs, MARIE *and* WANDA *hear the noise, but* MARIE *snorts with disgust and flounces over to* STEVE*'s bed, takes a half-pint bottle of scotch from her purse and drinks from the neck of the bottle.*

Downstairs, O.D. *has grabbed onto* STEVE, *holding him for support and using his superior weight and strength to bring him down. By clutching* STEVE *about the neck and shoulders he has reduced* STEVE*'s blows to the area of his midriff.*

STEVE *breaks away and lands two good blows upon* O.D.*'s face, but the larger man clumsily swings and knocks* STEVE *down. Now frightened,* STEVE *tries to scramble away but* O.D. *rushes him and slams him against the wall and butts him.*

STEVE *feebly punches, but* O.D. *brushes it aside and lands a right hand to* STEVE's *body that knocks the wind out of him.*

Then O.D. *grabs him like a rag doll and begins strangling him, bearing him down under his weight, until he straddles* STEVE *upon the floor and strangles him with all his returning strength.*)

VELMA

O.D. . . . no . . . no, O.D. . . . NO, O.D.! . . . NO! . . . NO! O.D.! . . . Please please please . . .

TOOTSIE (*Sensing* STEVE's *end*)

O.D., man . . . let him go. Hey, man . . . he's had enough . . . he can't defend himself, O.D. . . . Why don't cha let him up?

(*Frightened*)

But, O.D., man . . . you cut her . . . you cut her, man. . . . You know that was wrong, man. . . . Let him go, O.D. . . .

(O.D. *realizes that* STEVE's *not breathing any longer.*

He stands but wobbles on unfirm legs, then stares at VELMA *and stumbles over and slaps her off her chair.*

She crouches on the floor silently, covering her head with her hands and arms for protection.)

O.D. (*Over her*)

I should step on your head . . . bitch!

(TOOTSIE *has revived* STEVE *enough to cough and vomit. He pulls* STEVE *to his feet and half-carries him out onto the porch and they start up the stairs.*)

STEVE (*Gasping*)

Tootsie . . . hey, man . . . see about Velma. . . . See about Velma, man.

TOOTSIE

Man . . . that woman's wit her ole man. . . . Can't you understand that?

(O.D. *roughly drags* VELMA *from the floor as the lights go out downstairs.*)

STEVE (*Coughs, dizzy, at top of stairs*)

Next time . . . man, next time . . . I'll do it the right way.

TOOTSIE

Next time! Nigger, I sho wish I knew what goes on in yo' head.

WANDA (*Comes out and helps*)

What happened to Steve? Is that what all that noise was about?

(*They help him in.* MARIE *sits up in* STEVE's *bed.*)

Where's Marc, Tootsie? Is he all right?

MARIE

Damn . . . what caught hold of you, nigger? . . . You don't look good enough for an undertaker.

TOOTSIE

Marc's okay . . . he just took a run around the block . . .
heee heee heee. . . . 'N it wasn't fo' exercise neither . . .
hee ha ha ha . . .

(MONTGOMERY *enters the porch from the street and
walks into the open door to upstairs and begins
climbing the stairs.*)

MONTGOMERY (*Calls out as he climbs*)

Hey, ev'vabody! Grab yo cards, whiskey 'n women! It's party
time! . . . 'cause ole Montgomery . . . Saltsprings . . .
Henderson . . . just blew in!

BLACKNESS

DATE DUE

DEC 0 4 1990			